CROYDON
PAST

Looking north from the top of the Wellesley Road multi-storey car park in March 2002. The road has not been widened beyond this point. St Mary's Roman Catholic Church is on the right and Spurgeon's Tabernacle is beyond in the centre distance. In the right background is Grange Wood, a surviving part of the Great North Wood. One of Croydon's new trams is in the foreground.

CROYDON
PAST

JOHN GENT

Phillimore

2002

Published by
PHILLIMORE & CO. LTD.
Shopwyke Manor Barn, Chichester, West Sussex

© John Gent, 2002

ISBN 1 86077 223 4

Printed and bound in Great Britain by
BIDDLES LTD.
Guildford, Surrey

Contents

List of Illustrations

Frontispiece: Wellesley Road, 2002

Front endpaper: Croydon High Street, looking north, 1830
Back endpaper: Bath and West of England Agricultural Show at Croydon, 1875

Acknowledgements

MY INTEREST in Croydon's history was first stimulated in about 1943 by my form-master at Selhurst Grammar School, Kenneth Malcolm King ('Smiler'). In later visits to Croydon Reference Library, Kenneth Ryde and his successor, Peter Glover, encouraged my interest. The present Local Studies Librarian, Steve Roud, and his staff, particularly Christine Corner, Margaret Mumford and Grace Woutersz, have been most helpful with my preparations for this publication.

Peter Walker has spent hours at his computer producing a number of very useful maps and his input has been invaluable. He, Mike Hutchins, Steve Roud, Paul Sowan and Ron Cox have read through the manuscript and made a number of useful suggestions and comments for which I am very grateful.

I must also mention long-past local historians such as John Corbet Anderson, John Ollis Pelton, Clarence Paget and Ronald Bannerman, whose publications encouraged my early enthusiasm for local history and have greatly assisted this one.

Finally, my thanks go to Dave Smith (Memories of Hendon) for the excellent copies he has made from faded original photographs, and to Michael Noone for his general assistance.

THE ILLUSTRATIONS are from the following sources and permission for their reproduction is gratefully acknowledged:

Croydon Advertiser, 139, 150, 154; Croydon Natural History and Scientific Society, 25; Croydon Local Studies Library, 2, 3, 8, 11, 13-17, 20-4, 26, 30, 32, 33, 36, 38, 39, 41, 42, 44-9, 51-4, 56-60, 63, 65, 68, 71-3, 75-80, 82, 83, 85, 86, 92, 94, 95, 97, 102, 103, 105, 106, 108, 109, 113, 122, 123, 135, 140, 141, 144, 145, 148; John Gent, 7, 9, 12, 29, 35, 81, 153, 155-7; John Gent Collection, 4, 5, 10, 18, 19, 27, 28, 34, 37, 40, 43, 55, 61, 62, 64, 66, 69, 70, 74, 84, 87-91, 93, 98-100, 104, 107, 110-12, 116-21, 124-34, 136-8, 142, 147, 149, 152; Tim Harding, 146; Ken Maggs, 50; Tony Moss Collection, 114; Stuart Pickford, 151; Tom Samson, 158; Peter Walker, 1, 6, 31, 67, 96, 101, 115, 143.

Introduction

CROYDON is a very large town, with a population of 313,510 in 1991. It would be virtually impossible to write a fully comprehensive history. Over the years numerous books have been written on various aspects of the town. In this one I have attempted to collect together and edit information researched by myself and others over many years which is not easily available to the present-day reader. Some contemporary writers and documents have been quoted at length in an attempt to show what the town and life therein were like many years ago. Only 150 years ago Croydon was a country town set among some of the most beautiful countryside south of London. Agriculture was its main source of trade and in the following pages I have tried to demonstrate some of the influences that have made the town we know today. Although it grew fast and was totally transformed in a century from small market town to large residential and industrial suburb, the countryside was and still is on its doorstep.

Most of the illustrations have not been published in a book before but in a few cases, where there is only a very limited amount of material available, it has been necessary to use familiar images. Croydon is fortunate in the large amount of illustrative material available. Its library was established in 1890 as one of the first in the county of Surrey. In 1902 the Photographic Record and Survey of Surrey was formed and housed at Croydon Library, which also started its own collection of local photographs. This now amounts to some 40,000 images. My own collection of postcards and photographs now numbers around 15,000 and together these form an important local archive.

The present London Borough includes four ancient parishes with medieval churches. The parish of Croydon was altered when borough status was achieved in 1883 by removing Selsdon, a detached part known as Croydon Crook. This was then added to Sanderstead

parish. In 1915 Coulsdon and Purley Urban District Council was formed to include the old parishes of Coulsdon and Sanderstead. Then in 1928 Addington was added to what had become the County Borough of Croydon. Finally, in 1965 London government reorganisation merged the Croydon and Coulsdon and Purley areas to form one of the new London Boroughs.

In this publication I have concentrated on the area of the ancient parish, and later borough, of Croydon, but have not ignored the additions, which really justify books of their own. There is very little suitable illustrative material available from the period before the 1800s and because the greatest changes occurred after 1800 I have devoted more space to the two centuries since. Today much of the district is built over, but large areas of open space, woodland and downland remind us of a largely lost landscape. Many of the roads and footpaths follow the same alignment as those used by our forbears hundreds of years ago. A few old buildings which survive largely unchanged would be familiar to Croydonians of the past if they could return to visit the town today.

Stand at the crossroads in the centre of the town, at the corner of North End and George Street, and look down steep Crown Hill. The 15th-century tower of the parish church of St John the Baptist rises as a landmark above the shops in Church Street as it has for some 600 years. On the right is the Whitgift Hospital of the Holy Trinity still giving a home to old people from the parishes of Lambeth and Croydon as it has for the last 400 years. The scene would not be completely unfamiliar to any one of the last 15 to 20 generations of Croydonians, but they would recognise very little else in the city-scale town centre of the new century. They would almost certainly gaze in wonder at the new electric trams gliding past every few minutes.

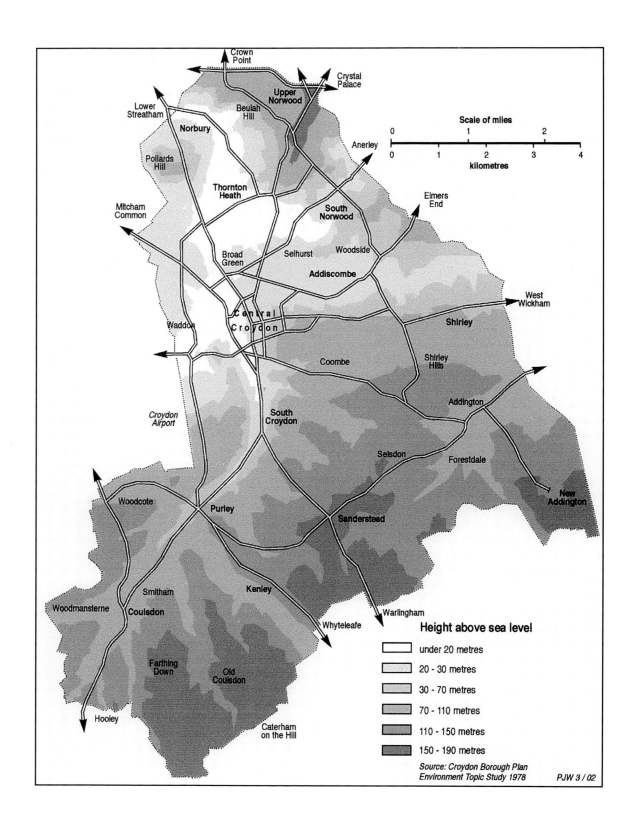

Crown Point

Crystal Palace

Upper Norwood

Lower Streatham

Beulah Hill

Norbury

Pollards Hill

Anerley

Thornton Heath

Mitcham Common

South Norwood

Broad Green

Selhurst

Woodside

Addiscombe

Elmers End

Central Croydon

Waddon

West Wickham

Shirley

Coombe

Shirley Hills

Croydon Airport

South Croydon

Addington

Selsdon

Forestdale

New Addington

Woodcote

Purley

Sanderstead

Smitham

Kenley

Woodmansterne

Coulsdon

Whyteleafe

Warlingham

Farthing Down

Old Coulsdon

Hooley

Caterham on the Hill

Scale of miles

0   1   2

0   1   2   3   4
kilometres

Height above sea level

under 20 metres

20 - 30 metres

30 - 70 metres

70 - 110 metres

110 - 150 metres

150 - 190 metres

*Source: Croydon Borough Plan
Environment Topic Study 1978*   PJW 3 / 02

I

Location and Background

THE SETTLEMENT of Croydon grew up just to the north of a gap through the North Downs. The downs are here at their highest (882 feet, 265 metres above sea level) and widest (about seven miles). A number of deep dry valleys meet to the south and early trackways no doubt converged on the place where there rose springs feeding the River Wandle.

The early history of Croydon is very obscure. The area has few significant field monuments but evidence of human occupation ten to eight thousand years ago has been found in the Wandle valley and on the surrounding downlands. From

about 1000 BC finds of flints, pottery, animal bones and metalwork mark small scattered settlements at Park Hill, and in the Wandle valley at Beddington and Waddon. Hoards of bronze implements found at Shirley, Addington, Purley, Coulsdon, Beddington and Carshalton suggest trading by itinerant smiths probably based on the important Bronze-Age site at what became Queen Mary's Hospital, Carshalton. Occupation continued at Park Hill, Beddington and at Waddon up to the Roman period, and at the Atwood School site in Sanderstead, where there was a larger settlement dating from the first century BC to the first century AD.

In Croydon town centre a Roman period settlement is suggested by the scattered finds of Roman coins and pottery, and a small amount of building material and metalwork. A small group of Roman-type burials and the likelihood of other undated skeletons being of the same period is a further pointer. Four hoards of Roman coins dated between the second and fourth centuries AD add to the evidence but no foundations of buildings have been found.

A Roman road linked London and Portslade (Brighton). Its course followed almost exactly the present A23 between Brixton and Broad Green. The modern road wanders slightly from the precise line because sections of the road on the London Clay became impassable after the Romans left and traffic would deviate to take a drier course. South of Broad Green the alignment is in some doubt. It may have followed the present London Road, North End, High Street, South End and Brighton Road,

1 (facing page) Croydon stands on the southern border of the London Basin at the foot of the long dip slope of the North Downs, which are here at their widest and reach their highest point, 882 feet (265 metres) above sea level, at Botley Hill. Lower lying Tertiary formations overlie the downland chalk and are exposed in a northward progression across the borough, comprising, in ascending order, sands of the Thanet Beds, loams and clays of the Woolwich and Reading Beds and heavier clays of the London Clay. Pebble and sand of the Blackheath Beds largely replace the Woolwich and Reading Beds on the eastern side of the town, and owing to their greater resistance to erosion form higher ground (and extend further up the downland slope) as clearly seen at Addington Hills and Croham Hurst. High on the downs remnants of Tertiary Beds provide a thin covering of Clay-with-Flints. The Norwood ridge, a long narrow hill in London Clay which escaped erosion, is a dominant feature of northern Croydon, reaching 376 feet (113 metres) above sea level. The lesser Pollards Hill to the west is also prominent.

Meltwater drainage in the Ice Age carved an intricate system of deep narrow valleys in the downland slope. As the climate ameliorated they became dry and the Wandle was much reduced in length. The flint debris washed out of the downland dry valley system in the Ice Age remains. The modern town centre stands on the gravel of the Fairfield Terrace, with Old Town on the lower Mitcham Terrace.

Diversity of soils gives the borough a variety of landscape and vegetation: heath and birch/pine woodland on the Tertiary sands, mixed oak woodland on the clays, with beechwood and grassland on the chalk.

2 *Croydon Church in 1822, seen from the Bleaching Grounds. The stream on the right was fed by Harris' Mill Pond (see page 53).*

or, less likely, gone through the low-lying area by Handcroft Road, Old Town and Southbridge Road. Eventually it followed the line of Riddlesdown Road to cross the down and join the alignment of the present A22 Eastbourne Road near Old Barn Lane. To the east another Roman road, from London to Lewes, forms part of the old county boundary between Surrey and Kent (Croydon and Bromley).

Later occupation is shown by the large quantity of coins, pottery and metalwork found in Whitgift Street. Saxon pottery found here is no doubt a link with the fifth- and sixth-century Edridge Road cemetery nearby. This, with the cemeteries at Beddington and Mitcham, would have belonged to some of the earliest Saxon immigrants to this country.

It is assumed the Croydon Saxon settlement grew up in the Old Town area near the parish church, where there is evidence of a Saxon church. Later activity, shown by domestic debris and coins, hints at the possibility of a Saxon manor house, predecessor of the Old Palace, and, from the presence of Roman building material, an even earlier building. The abundant water supply here was attractive for settlement, but brought problems of flooding and disease. As early as the 13th century it was referred to as 'Le Eldetoun', suggesting that the main

settlement had already moved up the slope to the aptly named High Street area.

Sixth- and seventh-century graves on the downs at Sanderstead, Riddlesdown, Purley and Coulsdon indicate Saxon occupation; on Farthing Down there is an impressive cemetery where 40 burials were discovered under and between barrows. There are also traces of an earlier Romano–British field system. The name Croydon is of Saxon origin and is thought to mean 'Crooked, wooded valley', or 'the valley where wild saffron grows'. Some other local names date from the same period and a number, such as Woodside, Norwood and Selhurst, remind us of the once densely wooded nature of the district.

The other three ancient parishes now included within the London Borough of Croydon are mentioned in Domesday Book. Their locations and areas relative to Croydon can be seen from the parish boundaries plan on page 5.

Addington

Addington parish was of medium size, around 3,600 acres. The settlement grew up on the spring line in the valley between the infertile, pebble, Addington Hills to the north-west and the chalk of the North Downs to the south and seems to have consisted of two separate manors. In latter days the manor was

3 This view of Addington Church dates from about 1868, before the north aisle was added in 1876. The Victorians carried out various 'improvements' which have altered its character. Five archbishops of Canterbury were buried here.

4 Coulsdon Church of St John replaced a Saxon building in about 1250. It was greatly enlarged in the late 1950s to cope with the local population increase. This view dates from the 1920s.

what is now known as Addington Palace. Largely built in 1780, with grounds thought to have been laid out by 'Capability' Brown, the house was used by the archbishops of Canterbury as a country residence between 1808 and 1896. Five archbishops are buried in the churchyard. After use as a country club, the palace housed the Royal School of Church Music from 1954 until 1996. It has recently been restored and is again used as a country club.

The parish remained almost completely rural into the 20th century, the population rising from only 178 in 1801 to 691 in 1921. Some parts of it were then developed for housing, and in 1928 it became part of the County Borough of Croydon. Even as late as the 1950s there were still several working farms, but further development has urbanised much of the area.

Coulsdon

Coulsdon was a large parish of about 4,300 acres. Domesday Book mentions not only Coulsdon, but Watendone (near present-day Kenley), which also had a church although it did not function as a parish. The settlement of Coulsdon is high on the

5   All Saints' Church, Sanderstead dates from the mid-13th century. Sanderstead Court, to the right, was the manor house dating from about 1676. It was destroyed by fire in 1957.

downs about 600 feet above sea level. The downs are intersected by deep dry valleys. Much of the parish remained rural until the 20th century.

The area now known as Coulsdon was for centuries called Smitham Bottom. The railway station which opened there as late as 1904 was and is called Smitham but the surrounding district is now Coulsdon, the original settlement on the hill being known as Old Coulsdon. The population in 1801 stood at 420 and had increased to only 713 by 1851. After this, housing development began to spread along the valleys. By 1901 the population was 6,523, and had reached 28,423 in 1931, by which time the old village area was being submerged by building activity. From 1894 the parish came under Croydon Rural District Council until this was superseded by Coulsdon and Purley Urban District Council in 1915.

Sanderstead

This small parish of some 2,260 acres lay between Addington and Coulsdon. It extended from the Croydon valley up on to the downs. The settlement was at a height of about 570 feet above sea level.

The present church dates from the 13th century, but it is thought there was an earlier Saxon church which is not recorded in Domesday Book. The manor house was beside the church, and remained as Sanderstead Court until demolition after the Second World War, following neglect and a fire. Again, the parish was predominantly rural into the 20th century. The population in 1801 was 204, in 1851 it was 235, and in 1901 it was 859. By then parts of the parish lower down the hill near the railway station (opened in 1884) were being developed for housing. Further development took place up the hill and around the village so that by 1931 the population had reached 9,279. Selsdon, originally a detached part of Croydon parish, was added to Sanderstead when Croydon achieved borough status in 1883.

In 1894 Sanderstead became part of Croydon Rural District Council. This was abolished in 1915 and Coulsdon and Purley Urban District Council was formed. This in turn became part of the London Borough of Croydon in 1965.

II

Parish and Manors

PARISH BOUNDARIES in the early 19th century almost invariably coincided with those of Saxon estates. The plan of 19th-century Surrey parishes between the Kent boundary and Leatherhead shows that each parish was long and narrow, running from north to south. The main settlements developed along the spring line where the chalk and clay lands meet. The parishes included land suitable for pasture and woodland to the north, and chalk downland for grazing sheep to the south. In between, the more fertile land on a mix of soils was suitable for arable purposes. In common with the other 20 Surrey parishes between it and Guildford, Croydon followed this pattern but was

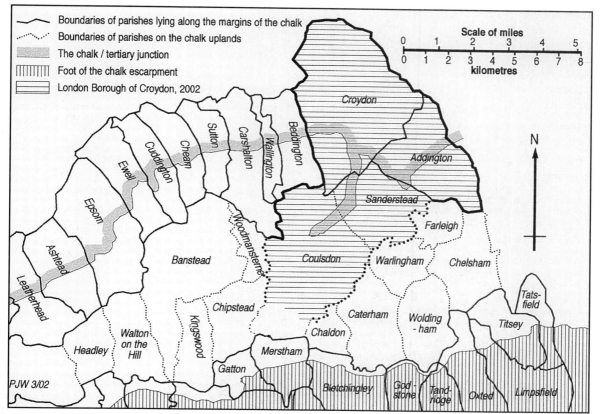

6 *The boundaries of Saxon estates often remained as parish boundaries until the Victorian period and have in many cases survived, at least in part, recent local government changes.*

7 (above)   Parish boundaries often followed tracks, streams or other recognisable physical features. Here, photographed in October 2001, a tiny stream and line of old oak trees form the boundary between Croydon (right) and Lambeth (left) at Norwood Grove, just as they have for centuries.

8 (right)   For centuries it was customary to perambulate parish boundaries to ensure they were known to the parishioners. In Croydon this was usually done in Rogation week (at intervals of a few years) under the direction of the vicar. The starting point was at Mill Lane, near Waddon Mill, that being the nearest point on the boundary to the parish church. The procession followed the sun in its course round the parish which took two days. At certain places the company halted while the vicar read a gospel, and boys were beaten as a way of instilling the positions of the boundary marks in their memories for later years. As some compensation for the indignities they suffered it was customary to present the boys with handfuls of 'Points', the tagged laces which were used to fasten clothes before buttons were in use.

*   Famous boundary marks were Elder Oak (Penge), Psalm Oak (Purley) and Vicar's Oak, at the top of what is now Anerley Hill. This photograph was taken on 28 May 1908 at the site of Vicar's Oak, which had long since been cut down. Those in the party included Henry Keatley Moore (extreme right) and the vicar (Rev. Leslie Burrows, just to the left of centre background). He was later to become Bishop of Lewes and then Bishop of Sheffield). The ceremony, known as 'Beating the Bounds', has not been performed in Croydon since 1927. The availability of well-researched maps has rendered the old custom unnecessary.*

at least twice the size of any of the others. This may reflect its importance as a possession of the archbishops, who owned it from at least the ninth century. In *Medieval Surrey*, John Blair suggests that, as several manors in this area were in Kentish hands, this part of Surrey may well have been part of Kent at one time. He also surmises that Croydon may well have been a minster church from which priests were sent out to more isolated and heathen parts of the area. A synod took place at Croydon in 809 and this supports the theory that it was a place of some religious importance. By the Middle Ages Croydon was the centre of a rural deanery and the church was one of the largest in the county.

Domesday Book records Croydon as belonging to Archbishop Lanfranc. There was a church and a mill. The population at that time is estimated at 365. It is apparent from this that the large parish of some 10,000 acres was very sparsely populated. Any importance the place had was later derived from the archbishops who, as lords of the manor, used their house as a staging point on journeys between London and Canterbury. Such journeys could not be undertaken quickly by the archbishop and his large retinue, and suitable resting places were needed *en route*. Croydon was only one of a chain of manor houses between 10 and 15 miles apart, but being near London it was also convenient as a country residence. Set amidst clear trout streams and wooded lands, with a deer park at nearby Park Hill, it offered the seclusion necessary from the responsibilities of state.

9 *This view of Oaks Lane, Shirley on 22 October 2001 shows how many of the local roads and lanes would have looked centuries ago. The road is shown on the Enclosure Map (page 33) but is now private and at this point crosses Shirley Park Golf Course, which was farmland until the early 20th century. Oaks Farm is in the distance.*

By around the 10th century the country was divided into 'Hundreds', administrative divisions whose influence declined as parochial, manorial and judicial bodies became more important. It is thought the areas originally contained a hundred families or a hundred taxable hides of land. A hide was the amount of land that could be ploughed in a year using an eight-ox team. This varied with the soil quality but was between 60 and 180 acres. Croydon was situated in Wallington Hundred which suggests that the neighbouring settlement was at one time more important. Later it became known as Croydon Hundred. The Hundred Courts remained in existence until local government changes in the late 19th century.

The manor house, or Croydon House as it was then known, was originally used as an administrative centre for the archbishops' estates in the area. The archbishops are thought to have visited from the 12th century onwards and it is known that King Henry III was there at least eight times between 1229 and 1264. The manor house was gradually enlarged and further domestic buildings were added to make it suitable for the many distinguished guests who visited the archbishops. Monarchs staying here included the first three Edwards, Henry IV, Henry VI, Henry VII, Mary and Elizabeth I. In August and September 1556, 23 meetings of the Privy Council took place there. The presence of members of the royal retinue and various officials, all requiring accommodation and refreshment, placed very severe demands on the town, but brought opportunities for local trade.

The manor house was the scene of some notable events. King James I of Scotland was imprisoned there for some time after July 1409, before being sent to the Tower of London. John Frith was tried for heresy by Archbishop Cranmer in 1533 and was later burnt at Smithfield. Queen Mary spent a month convalescing in 1556. Numerous bishops were consecrated there, and Sir Christopher Hatton received the Great Seal of England from the Queen in the Long Gallery on his appointment as Lord Chancellor.

By 1600 the manor was known as Croydon Palace, and after the impeachment of Archbishop Laud in 1640 the property was taken from the See of Canterbury and leased to Charles, Earl of Nottingham. From 1642 Civil War raged and in 1645 Laud was executed. In 1647 the estate was purchased by Sir William Brereton, commander of the Parliamentary forces at the siege of Chester. A Royalist pamphleteer described Sir William as 'a notable man at a thanksgiving dinner, having long teeth and a prodigious stomach to turn the archbishop's chapel at Croydon into a kitchen, also to swallow up that Palace as a morsel'. After Charles II was restored to the throne in 1660 the See of Canterbury repossessed Croydon Palace. Sir William Brereton

died at Croydon in 1661 and was buried here.

Archbishop Hutton was the last primate to use the palace, in 1757. The town had become more industrialised and less attractive and the palace was reputed to be unhealthy: 'in a low and unwholesome situation, incommodious and unfit to be a habitation of an Archbishop of Canterbury'. In 1780 the See of Canterbury obtained a private Act of Parliament to sell Croydon Palace. It was auctioned in 1781 and part became a factory for calico printing. Other parts were used for housing and as a school of industry. In 1830 the east wall of the Great Hall collapsed. Some of the land was gradually sold off, and several of the buildings were demolished. In the mid-1880s the fate of the remaining buildings was in the balance. It was hoped to buy it for the town, to commemorate Queen Victoria's Golden Jubilee, but subscriptions were insufficient. In 1887 the Duke of Newcastle bought the Palace and gave it to the Sisters of Mercy of the Church of England. They repaired much of the fabric and opened a girls school in 1889. After a century of loving care in their hands it is now part of the Whitgift Foundation and known as the Old Palace School of John Whitgift.

A large part of the buildings remain, unique among the former palaces of the archbishops. It is Croydon's most important building, both historically and architecturally, and is Grade I listed. Because it is in use as a school it is only open to the public for guided tours on a few days each year. The Great Hall, dating from the 14th/15th centuries, has a magnificent arch-braced roof. The Guard Room may have started as a late 12th-century first-floor hall but was remodelled as an audience chamber around 1400. The Chapel was probably built by Archbishop Bouchier between 1460 and 1480 but remodelled and lengthened by Archbishop Morton. The building has many other rooms and contains architecture from virtually every century from the 11th to 21st, with the latest extension in Tudor style opened in 2001.

Early local government was largely centred on the court of the Manor of Croydon. The matters

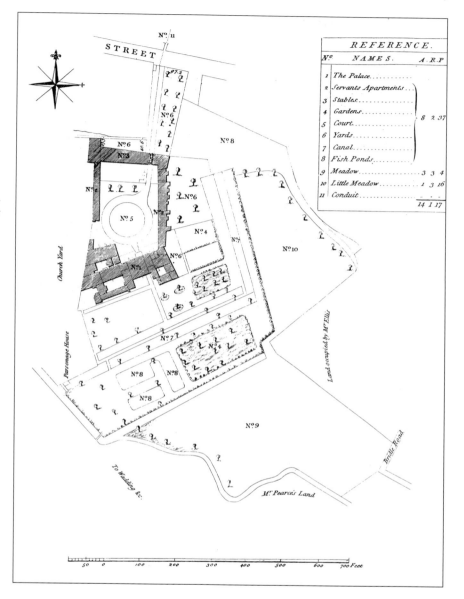

REFERENCE.

Nº	NAMES.	A.R.P
1	The Palace.............	
2	Servants Apartments...	
3	Stables...............	
4	Gardens..............	8 2 37
5	Court................	
6	Yards................	
7	Canal................	
8	Fish Ponds...........	
9	Meadow..............	3 3 4
10	Little Meadow.........	1 3 16
11	Conduit..............	- . -
		14 1 17

10 This plan of the Arch-bishop's Palace and Grounds dates from about 1780.

dealt with by this court were many. It issued regula-
tions to be observed by all who put cattle out to
graze on commons within the manor and settled
the fees to be paid to the common herdsman for
looking after them. It ordered that all properties
should be fenced in and imposed penalties for
non-observance of this rule. It 'stinted' the common
fields by limiting the number of beasts that could
be put out to graze on them. It also dealt with
obstruction of the streets and footpaths, and much
of its business was concerned with the transfer of
land.

Within the parish of Croydon there were a
number of sub-manors of various degrees of importance. The owners held these under the archbishop
as chief lord. Of those which are known to have
held courts the most northerly was Benchesham,
or Bensham, later, at least in part, known as Norbury.

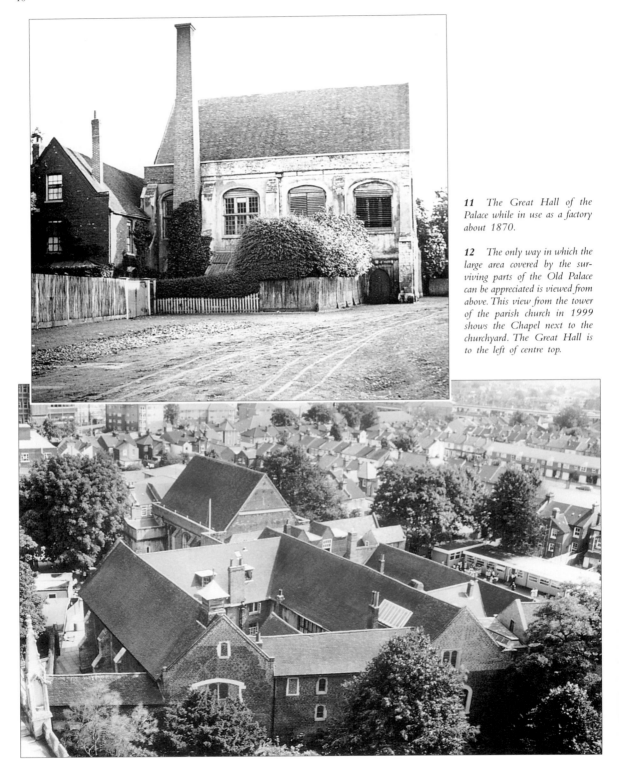

11 *The Great Hall of the Palace while in use as a factory about 1870.*

12 *The only way in which the large area covered by the surviving parts of the Old Palace can be appreciated is viewed from above. This view from the tower of the parish church in 1999 shows the Chapel next to the churchyard. The Great Hall is to the left of centre top.*

The Manor of Croham was to the south east and extended partly into Sanderstead parish, while to the south the Manor of Haling extended from Duppas Hill to the southernmost point of the parish at Purley. On the west was Waddon, while the Rectory Manor consisted of land just north of the town itself.

In 1493, when John Morton was Archbishop of Canterbury, one of the periodic surveys of the parish was conducted to assess the quit-rents to be paid annually by tenants. Quit-rent was a small sum paid in lieu of services which tenants might be called upon to perform for the lord of the manor. In *By-Ways in the History of Croydon*, Clarence Paget put together from this survey and other sources the following description of the parish at the time:

> Morton's surveyor starts in the neighbourhood of George Street, where he notes a few tenements and barns, and proceeds up North End and London Road, taking the land on the eastern side of the highway, which then consisted largely of enclosures of cultivated land. One of these was named Oakfield ... the name is preserved in our present Oakfield Road.
>
> Passing on to where now St. James Road meets the London Road we get a first glimpse of that great common, known as Croydon Heath, or Croydon Common, which at this point had a neck reaching to the London Road. Across this neck was a gate, known as Broad Green Gate, which served to prevent the numerous cattle which pastured on the common from straying on to the highway. Let us contemplate the common as we lean upon this gate. It contained about 280 acres and stretched from Selhurst on the east to Broad Green on the west, and from Whitehorse on the north to Cherry Orchard Road on the south. In front lies the gravel track which then represented Windmill Road and Northcote Road, running straight as a dart across the common to another gate on its far side, called Selhurst Gate ... A short distance along this road, sufficiently far to clear the enclosures which lined the London Road, branched off another long straight track, now the St. James Road and Lower Addiscombe Road, which left the common by a gate across the latter

> road, close to the point where Warren Road now enters it. On our left hand is the edge of the common gradually widening away from the Windmill Road track until it reaches another gate, known as Bensham Gate, which stood across what is now Whitehorse Road, not very far from its junction with Whitehorse Lane. This gate barred another straight road across the common, which was stopped at its further end by a gate, called New Gate, which spanned the Wellesley Road at a point some 150 yards south of where now stands Spurgeon's Bridge. Wellesley Road was then Newgate Lane ... There were in addition two more gates to the common; the one, Middleheath Gate, stood across the Sydenham Road ... and the other, Cony Lane Gate, spanned what is now Cherry Orchard Road, near the junction with Cross Road.
>
> Cattle feeding on Croydon Common were marked with C.C., the mark of the common, and a common herdsman was appointed from time to time to look after them. The herdsman's fee was a halfpenny for a horse or cow, and a penny for three colts or three bullocks, and if the fee was unpaid he was at liberty to drive the cattle of the defaulter to the pound, and keep them there until he was satisfied of his dues. Sheep were not encouraged upon Croydon Common, being barred therefrom from Candlemas Day (2 February) to St Andrew's Day (30 November) in each year.
>
> Continuing up London Road were the great common fields of Bensham, which were traversed diagonally by the ancient way, then as now called Bensham Lane. These fields extended as far as Colliers Water Lane ... On reaching that lane, Morton's surveyor turns back to his original starting point, and next takes the western side of London Road. Here the Rectory Manor of Croydon held privileges in respect of an area bounded by North End, London Road, Handcroft Road and Pitlake. Within it was the glebe land of the Rectory, containing about thirty acres, known as Parson's Mead, and also a small triangular common of four acres, called Broad Green, situated at the junction of Handcroft Road with London Road.
>
> Further along the London Road the highway passed across Thornton Heath, a common of about thirty acres, which stretched on both

sides of the road at Thornton Heath Pond to a point some 600 yards higher up. This heath, sometimes also known as Granden Heath, was the common of Norbury Manor, which adjoined it on its northern side. In Morton's survey that part of the Norbury estate which lay on the western side of the London Road is called Granden and Pollards Hill.

At Hermitage Bridge, on the western side of the road and just within our parish, was a small enclosure of land, known as Battle Close … Having reached the northern limit of the parish the surveyor now turns along Green Lane, then described as the way leading from the Hermitage to Whitehorse. There can be little doubt that a hermit's cell anciently existed close to this locality … Passing along Green Lane we may note on the left hand the ancient way, now called Gibson's Hill, but then Cupgate Lane. This lane, before it reached the top of the hill, opened out on to Norwood, and Cup Gate no doubt barred its entrance to the common. In all rather more than 900 acres of this great common lay within the parish. It stretched in length from Crown Lane on the north west to Woodside on the south east, and was about two-thirds of a mile in breadth. Across the common from end to end ran the gravel road now represented by Beulah Hill, South Norwood Hill and Portland Road.

Continuing our way along Green Lane we pass the Norbury estate on the right hand, with its old manor house, which stood near the spot where now Norbury and Kensington Avenues meet, and on the left the ancient farm of Biggen, which contained about 120 acres and extended to the edge of Norwood. Biggen Farm was bounded on the south side by the old thoroughfare known as Bewley Street [now Spa hill and Northwood Road]. On the south side of this road was a small farm of ten acres, which later, with the addition of some twenty acres of woodland, became the famous Beulah Spa.

Passing along what is now Parchmore Road, was an estate of less than a hundred acres, known as Pasmers, otherwise Tilehost. The name later became corrupted to Pasmore, or Parchmore. Just before reaching the junction of Parchmore Road with Brigstock Road (formerly part of Colliers Water Lane) was a small green called Walkers Green, which is now represented by

the increased width of roadway. From here we pass up what is now Thornton Heath High Street, and along Whitehorse Road, leaving on our left hand the manor house of Whitehorse, which stood slightly south-east of the junction of Whitehorse Road and Whitehorse Lane. Entering Croydon Common by Bensham Gate, and crossing a corner of it, we leave it again by Selhurst Gate, and go along Selhurst Road [then Selhurst Lane]. Near the site of Norwood Junction we pass on to the common of Norwood, and, turning to the right across that common, reach Woodside. Here is the ancient green, which alone survives of the many there once were in Croydon.

On our return journey to the town we pass along Blackhorse Lane, Lower Addiscombe Road, across Croydon Common to Cony Lane Gate, and so to Park Lane, then called Back Lane. The land on the eastern side of Park Lane was known as South Stakefield, from its position south of Stake Cross, which stood at the crossing of Park Lane with George Street. On the north-east corner of this crossing [where now is the underpass] stood the pound, and at the south-eastern corner the large field known as the Fair Field, in which for centuries Croydon Fair was held until it was abolished in 1868.

We next visit Addiscombe Road [then Addiscombe Lane], which was bordered on its southern side by Croydon Park, the property of the archbishop. The Park, which contained some 170 acres, extended over what is now Park Hill, and its vicinity to Coombe Road, and was formerly stocked with deer. Higher up the Addiscombe Road on its northern side was the Addiscombe Estate, and just beyond it on the same side of the road, a large common field, known as the Clays, through which in a diagonal direction ran to Stroud Green an ancient lane, which bore at the end of the eighteenth century the curious name of Slutts Hall Lane. Stroud Green was a small common of about twelve acres, which lay opposite Ashburton Park.

13 (facing page)   The parish church of St John the Baptist was one of the largest in Surrey. Seen here in 1860, it was largely destroyed in a disastrous fire in 1867. The original 15th-century tower remained and the rebuilt church, consecrated in 1870, is slightly larger. Six archbishops are buried here.

14   On the night of 5 January 1867 fire almost completely destroyed the parish church. The remains of the tomb of Archbishop Sheldon were among the ruins photographed here and were not restored until nearly 100 years later. Many other fine monuments were lost in the fire.

On the southern side of Addiscombe Road, opposite the Clays, lay another large common field, known as Upfield. To the south lay another common field, named Rippingill, and still further, between Rippingill and Coombe Road, yet another, called Coombe Field, which was later entirely absorbed by the Coombe House estate.

At the upper end of Coombe Road was another small common of about 18 acres, known as Broad Coombe, by the enclosure of which the estates of Coombe House and Coombe Lodge were appreciably increased. 'From Coombe we go by the road [Oaks Lane – now no longer a public highway – illustration 9] which led past the old farmhouse, still known as Coombe Farm, which brings us on to another large common, called Shirley Heath. This heath contained another 220 acres, and lay between the parish boundary and the Wickham Road, extending slightly beyond Shirley Road on the west. The village of Shirley lay on the northern side of the Wickham Road and overlooked the heath, whilst beyond it was the ancient estate of Ham Farm. Passing across Shirley Heath and Addington Hills and down Conduit Lane we arrive in Croham.

The Manor of Croham, which was divided in two in 1590, formerly included the land on either side of Croham Road down to South End. The original manor house was quite close to the town, possibly on the site of Blunt House, which stood near the present Aberdeen Road.

The valley in which Brighton Road runs was known as Smithden or Smitham bottom, and on its western side was the manor of Haling, which originally extended down as far as where now stands Christ Church Memorial Hall, and contained a large wood of 116 acres which crowned the ridge along which Pampisford Road now runs.

The Manor of Waddon, which completes our survey, lay on the western side of the parish, and contained on the north a common of about 220 acres, known as Waddon Marsh, which was traversed by the Mitcham Road, in the centre its village and the large estate of Waddon Court Farm, and on the south its great common fields stretching southwards of the Beddington Road, and ending at the extreme southern point of the parish with down land upon which sheep were pastured.

With the help of this description it is possible to imagine Croydon as it was between 500 and 200 years ago. Until the beginning of the 19th century the quiet country town was surrounded by fields, woods and furze-clad commons, dotted here and there with a tiny cottage, an ancient farm or a gentleman's house set in attractive parkland.

John Whitgift and his Legacy

JOHN WHITGIFT was born in about 1530. Having been Master of Trinity College, Cambridge, and having served as Vice-Chancellor of the University, he was consecrated Bishop of Worcester in 1577 and Archbishop of Canterbury in 1583. While spending much of his time at Lambeth, he also became very fond of Croydon, which he would visit as much as possible.

Whitgift became relatively wealthy and decided to found a hospital. In 1594 he purchased an old inn, the *Chequer*, at the corner of North End and George Street. He also acquired several other properties to provide an endowment for the hospital, or almshouse. It was intended for the maintenance of poor Christians, was to be called the Hospital of the Holy Trinity, and was to consist of a warden and poor to any number under forty. The plan and arrangement were to resemble those of a Cambridge college, with staircases giving access to rooms on two floors. In 1597/8 Whitgift bought further property to add to his endowment, including land at Ryecrofts and Christian Fields in Norwood, and at Stroud Green. In 1599 further extensive property was purchased including farms at Woodside, Shirley and Addiscombe, and the Croham Manor estate. More small purchases and gifts over the ensuing few years gave the Whitgift Foundation valuable assets which have contributed to making it what must now be one of the richest charitable foundations in the country.

Whitgift also provided a school and schoolmaster's house in George Street. The foundation stones of the hospital were laid on 22 March 1596

15 *John Whitgift was born in about 1530 and consecrated Bishop of Worcester in 1577. He became Archbishop of Canterbury in 1583. Upon his death in 1604 he was buried at Croydon.*

and this date is always kept as Founder's Day. The hospital was completed in 1599 and the school in 1600. The latter seems to have flourished for some time but no provision had been made for a governing body, the vicar of Croydon being the supervisor of both school and hospital. By the end of the 18th century the schoolhouse appears to have fallen into disuse.

As a result of the Enclosure Act a further 110 acres of former common land was added to the

foundation's property in 1801. By 1812 a National School had been established in the schoolhouse, and during the following decades a group of influential local residents, dissatisfied with the situation, managed to get the newly formed Charity Commissioners to agree to establish a Court of Governors. A new 'Poor School' would be built in Church Road. This opened in 1858, the pupils from the National School being transferred there. The 'Middle Class School' in North End, which at that time was known simply as Whitgift School, did not open until 1871, under the headmastership of Robert Brodie. The original schoolhouse was by now in use as a store.

The Elizabethan schoolhouse and headmaster's house were unfortunately demolished in the late 1890s. If Croydon Corporation had got its way the almshouses would have gone too, for road widening. After years of dispute, in which various preservation and learned societies were involved, the House of Lords settled the matter by striking out a clause permitting demolition from the Croydon Corporation Bill of 1923. The Grade I listed building remains to serve its original purpose, and is a haven of peace in the heart of the town.

16 (above left)   In this view of North End in 1833, the Whitgift Hospital is on the right, with the Crown inn on the left. There was a public pump in the middle of George Street.

17 (above)   This drawing shows Whitgift's Elizabethan Schoolhouse and the Headmaster's House in George Street. These fine historic buildings were sadly demolished around 1899. Allders' George Street frontage now occupies the site.

18 (above right)   The Whitgift Middle School in Church Road about 1910. It dated from 1855 and was demolished in the early 1930s.

19 (right)   This aerial view shows the Whitgift School in North End about 1924. When the new school was opened at Haling Park this replaced the Church Road school. It was demolished in 1965 and the Whitgift Centre now occupies the site.

The Poor School in Church Road was closed in 1881 and reopened in 1882 as the Whitgift Middle School. The North End school was relaunched as Whitgift Grammar School. This moved in 1931 to new premises at Haling Park in South Croydon and the Middle School moved from Church Road to the North End site. By the 1950s the Middle School had been renamed the Trinity School of John Whitgift, and in 1965 it moved to new buildings at Shirley Park, the valuable North End site being transformed into the Whitgift Shopping Centre.

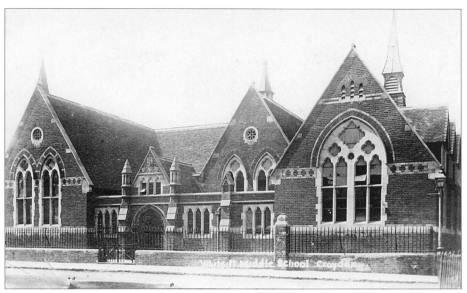

20   *Haling House was demolished to provide a site for the new Whitgift School, which opened in 1931. Haling is first mentioned in 1202 and in 1536 it was in the possession of Hugh Warham. In 1592 the manor was granted to Charles, Lord Howard of Effingham, England's High Admiral at the time of the Spanish Armada, who lived there until his death in 1624. The weather vane surmounting the 1931 school buildings is, appropriately, in the form of a Spanish galleon.*

Until after the Second World War conditions in the Whitgift Hospital were best described as primitive, with outside communal toilets and water obtainable only from a tap in the courtyard. This was remedied and the single-room accommodation changed to two rooms, with modern facilities. The audience chamber on the first floor remains virtually unchanged from Whitgift's day.

In 1988 Whitgift House, a new home for the elderly, was opened at Haling Park. Responsibility for the Old Palace School passed to the Whitgift Foundation in 1993 and it is now known as the Old Palace School of John Whitgift. The name of this Elizabethan archbishop is, quite rightly, well-known in the town he loved and which his generosity has benefited more than he could possibly have imagined.

IV

The Seventeenth and Eighteenth Centuries

THE FIRST CENSUS took place in 1801, but fairly detailed Taxation Returns show that the population of Croydon was about 1,000 in 1332 and had risen to about 2,700 by 1673. There were three early grants to Croydon of markets and fairs. The first, in 1276, granted Archbishop Kilwardby a weekly market on Wednesday, and a nine-day fair; the second was a grant in 1314 to Archbishop Reynolds for a weekly market on Thursday and a three-day fair around St Matthew's Day; and the third a grant to Archbishop Stratford in 1343 for a weekly market on Saturday and a fair. These markets and fairs probably already existed, but official recognition enabled the lord of the manor to collect tolls. The Saturday market and the fairs survived until the 19th century. In 1566 a property was conveyed to trustees with a requirement that it should 'for ever be wholly used for a common markett house, or place for the ease of the people resorting to the markett'. This was probably opposite the *Greyhound* in the High Street, later the site of the Butter Market.

In 1609 Francis Tyrrell, citizen and grocer of London, left £200 to a trustee to 'cause to be newe built, erected and set up with the same a newe market house upon the ould markett hill in Croydon, where the cage now standeth'. A building known as the Cornmarket House or Great Market was duly erected. After later rebuilding, it was demolished in 1808. It is regarded as the first town hall.

Corn, cattle and sheep were the principal commodities sold in the market, and a fishmarket was held in Middle Row which was sometimes referred to as Fishmarket Street, Old Fish Street, or the Fishmarket. Fees known as quarterages, stackage and stallage were due to the archbishop or to whoever he might assign the right to collect the dues. Farmers from 'below hill' (as those from the south side of the downs were described) often brought their grain into Croydon on days other than market days, and stored it in rooms in the local inns, selling it to customers either in or outside the market from samples in their pockets, thus avoiding the tolls. The *Ship* in the High Street had such a room upstairs. Where the grain was pitched in the market the toll-gatherer would thrust his 'dish' (which held a quart of grain) into every sack and put it into a tub, then sell it when sufficient had accumulated.

The main inns in Croydon in the 17th century were the *Swan*, on the site now occupied by Allders, the *Crown*, opposite the Whitgift Hospital, the *George*, on the site of the Natwest Bank and, between there and the present *Ship*, the *Cross Keys* at the corner of Park Street, the *Greyhound*, the *Red Lion*, the *Kings Arms* and the *White Lion*. There were a number of others in the market area.

Apart from brewing and agricultural trades, the principal industry of Croydon at this time was probably charcoal burning. With a plentiful supply of wood, the area was a main source of fuel for London in the days before coal was brought down from the north-east of England by boat. Greene, in his *Quip for an Upstart Courtier* published in 1592, has the following line: 'Marry, quoth hee that lookt like Lucifer, though I am black, I am not the Divell, but indeed a collyer of Croydon.' A comedy entitled *Grim, the Collier of Croydon, or the Devil and his Dame, with the Devil and St Dunstan, by J.T.* was published in 1662. A poem by Patrick Hannay, published in 1662, gives a somewhat unfavourable description of the town:

This place I say doth border on a plaine,
Which Step-dame Nature seemes t'have made
    in scorne,
Where hungrie husbandmen have toild in vaine,
And with the share the barren soile have torne;
Nor did they rest till rise of ruddie morne:
Yet when was come the harvest of their hopes,
They for their gaine doe gather grainless crops;

It seemes of starv'd sterilitie the seat,
Where barren downes do it inviron round;
Whose parched tops in summer are not wet,
And only are with snow in winter crown'd,
Only with barrenesse they doe still abound;
Or if on some of them we roughness finde,
It's towny heath, badge of the barren rinde.

In midst of these stands CROYDON cloath'd in
    blacke,
In a low bottome sinke of all these hills;
And is receipt of all the durtie wracke,
Which from their tops still in abundance trils.
The unpav'd lanes with muddie mire it fills,
If one shower fall, or if that blessing stay,
You may well smell, but never see your way.

For never doth the flowre-perfumed aire,
Which steals choice sweets from other blessed
    fields,
With panting breast take any resting there,
Nor of that prey a portion to it yields,
For those harsh hills his comming either shields,
Or else his breath infected with their kisses
Cannot enrich it with his fragrant blisses.

And those who there inhabit, suiting well
With such a place, doe either nigro's seeme
Or harbingers for Pluto, prince of hell;
Or his fire-beaters one might rightly deeme,
Their sight would make a soull of hell to dreame;
Besmear'd with sut, and breathing pitchie smoake,
Which, save themselves, a living wight would
    choke.

21   Charcoal burners in the Great North Wood.

Charcoal burning locally seems to have died out by the late 18th century, but Colliers Water Lane in Thornton Heath is a reminder of this once important local industry.

Croydon did not escape the effects of the plague during the 17th century. The parish registers record 158 deaths in 1603/4, 76 in 1625, 24 in 1626 and 74 in 1631. In 1665/6 there were 141 deaths from the plague.

From 1660 until 1684 the townspeople suffered from another sort of plague – their vicar. William Clewer was appointed by Archbishop Juxon on the recommendation of Charles II, who did not realise his true character. Clewer was a great persecutor of the Royalists during the Commonwealth and enjoyed the living of Ashton in Northamptonshire, to which he had been appointed when about 18 and, according to Walker's *List of the Ejected Clergy*, 'was of a very ill life and very troublesome to his neighbours'. He was once tried and burnt in the hand at the Old Bailey for stealing a silver cup. The following extracts are from *The Case of the Inhabitants of the Town and Parish of Croydon, in the County of Surrey, concerning the great Oppressions they ly under, by reason of the unparalleled Extortions, and violent, illegal, and unwarrantable Prosecutions of Doctor William Clewer, Vicar of the said Parish: Humbly presented to the consideration of Parliament* – 1673:

That the said Doctor by unjust, vexatious and numerous suits, by him frequently brought against his parishioners, extorts more from them than what either his predecessors claimed or had, or is his due.

… He frequently, after he hath been paid his full dues, arrests his poor parishioners, and forces them to pay the same over again; together with great sums for charges, which he pretends he hath been at; declaring he will have of them what he pleases, for he cannot live on his dues.

… Several poor people having, in the time of the late dreadful sickness, buried relations in the woods, the said Doctor, in the time of their necessity, was so far from extending his charity towards their relief, that he forced them to pay unreasonable fees for their burials, as if they

had been buried by him in the church-yard. Those that would not comply with him, he sued and extorted great sums of money from them, for his charges as well as duties, before he would clear his persecution.

… He, by his violent persecution of diverse poor men, hath forced them to leave their wives and children, and seek shelter in remote places, to the utter ruine of their families.

… He hath arrested several on pretended great actions, and thereby kept them in prison, and yet, on the trial, could prove nothing against them, to the utter ruin of these poor people imprisoned; and hath forced several persons to pay him five pounds, when his due is but twelve pence.

By these and like extortions he makes his living worth above £250 per annum, which never was worth, to any of his predecessors, above £60, and he enricheth himself by the ruin of his parishioners, especially the poorer sort, that live on the common, whom he endeavours to enslave, because they are not able to contend with him at law.'

At a meeting of the Court of Whitehall, in the presence of the King, further details were requested from the parishioners and duly submitted, and put before a further meeting of the Council in April 1673. The following statement was included:

… That, when as the sacrament money hath been collected for the poor, he took a third part of it to his own use, saying 'None was poorer than the vicar' and kept it; which hath since prevented men's charity.

… He hath caused the gentry to leave the towne, to the ruin thereof; spoiled the school, so that no gentlemen came to it. He hath caused lands and houses to fall in their rents; brought down the price of them, in their sale, above three years' purchase; makes tenants that they will take no lease, unless landlords will covenant to secure against him; which they dare not do; and so the houses and lands stay empty, and lie waste. And he hath forced the parishioners to leave their parish church, and to keep from receiving the sacrament; insomuch that there are not above ten or twelve in all (beside

23 *This Market House was built at the expense of Francis Tyrrell, grocer and citizen of London. It is regarded as Croydon's first town hall and stood near the corner of High Street and Butcher Row (now Surrey Street). Market houses were often used for parochial business which led to their being called town halls. It was replaced by a new Town Hall in 1809.*

alms-people, who are obliged), that will come to the church or sacrament; but if a stranger at any time do preach, there come at least six, seven, or eight hundred.

The King and Court then referred the whole matter to the Archbishop of Canterbury, who with the Lord Chancellor met to hear both parties at Lambeth House (one of the Archbishops' palaces). Further complaints were put including: 'That the said Doctor Clewer was a notorious and common thief, that used to come into bookseller's shops and steal books, and carry them away ...' The parishioners came up with a proposal to rid themselves of Clewer by paying him a settled maintenance of £160 per annum, effectively to stay away from the town. The Archbishop and Lord Chancellor thought this reasonable, but before the next hearing by the Court,

> unluckily it fell out, that Dr Clewer, having taken a little too much of the creature, in London, being upon his journey home, just as

22 (facing page) John Rocque's one-inch map of Surrey including the Croydon area dates from 1765. It is a reasonable representation of the area and some of the road names are still in use.

God would please to have it (to show what he deserved), against the gallows, near Newington Butts, his horse threw him, or he fell off from his horse, broke his leg in three pieces, and put his shoulder out. There he lay, and none would help him, the people thereabouts knowing him so well, that one cried, 'There lies the vicar of Croydon, with his leg broke; I would to God he had broken his neck; the church would then be no more scandalized by such a rogue, nor the poor people tormented.'

Others wished more severe things, which savoured not of Christianity; therefore we will not mention them; but certain it is, no one would help to remove him till they were paid beforehand, because he is counted so great a knave that none would trust him; nor would a coachman take him up to carry him to Dr. Welden's house [the parson of Newington], before he had ten shillings in hand, which is not half a mile ...

During his sickness, Clewer was asked by the Archbishop if he would resign. He declared 'that he would, so soon as there were indifferent persons nominated to arbitrate the differences between him and the parishioners, concerning arrears of tithes.' The Archbishop and Lord Chancellor appointed

Sir Adam Brown and Sir William Haward to arbitrate on the matter. They met on several occasions at the *George* inn, Doctor Clewer repeatedly putting obstacles in their way by turning up late, feigning sickness, claiming he had forgotten, or refusing to turn up at all. Sir William and Sir Adam's report to the Archbishop and Lord Chancellor concluded as follows:

> … And, having thus proceeded (being weary with these delays), we left the said parishioners, who most humbly and unanimously implore your good Lordship's favour to remove from them the said Doctor, and that a good man be placed amongst them. In which suit we also humbly join to your honours, as a thing which for the reasons aforesaid, we do judge very convenient; all which, nevertheless, we humbly submit to your Lordships' judgements.

The Archbishop and Lord Chancellor then agreed to do all they could to remove Doctor Clewer, but after promising he would resign he continued in his old ways:

> … but the Doctor, resolving to persist in his villainies to ruin the parish of Croydon (as he frequently declares he will do before he leaves it), refuses to surrender, but continues to go on in horrid oppressions and vexations, commencing suits against his parishioners, without colour of cause to their unspeakable damage.
>
> Under these sad oppressions, the poor parish having lain these thirteen years languishing, they now become humble supplicants to the Parliament of England, to enable them by an Act to give such maintenance to a succeeding minister as may be an encouragement to a sober, learned, orthodox and peaceable man to come and settle amongst them; to do the church that right as to remove so wicked and scandalous a person out of it; and for the honour and vindication of the religion of the Church of England, to make him for ever incapable of serving in the church again; than which no greater advantage can be done to the Church of England at this time.
>
> For the said Doctor is a frequenter of houses of debauchery, particularly a blind, beggarly, disorderly ale-house, in a byplace within the parish of Newington, notoriously infamous for

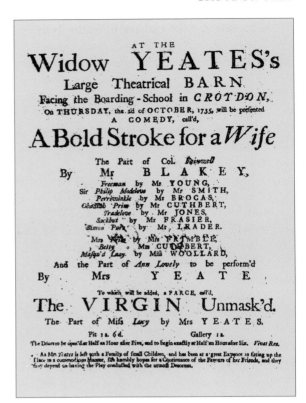

24 *This handbill is the first record of a theatrical performance in Croydon. The location of the barn is not known.*

entertainment of lewd persons, where the officers (having notice given them) about midnight found him (upon search) hid in a garret, and were carrying him to the counter or prison in the Borough, till he discovered himself to be a clergyman, and besought their civility, entreating that they would not disgrace him publicly; whereupon they released him. But the house soon after was in danger to be pulled down for a baudy-house.

It is humbly submitted, whether this man be fit to be continued in the Church, or to be made a public example, to deter other clergymen from such wicked practices for the future.

It seems incredible that it was a further ten years before the town was rid of Dr Clewer, who was not ejected from his post until 1684. Perhaps this was the meaning of a perpetual curacy. Once a vicar was appointed to a living it needed an Act of Parliament to be rid of him.

Successive Acts of Parliament in the 16th and 17th centuries encouraged the transformation of the parish, through its meetings of the vestry, into a secular authority. The long-standing duty of levying a church rate was now supplemented by the requirement that rates for poor relief and for the upkeep of the highways should be levied as well. The manor courts declined in importance except in connection with land transfers and inheritance. Most vestries were open, and any male ratepayer could attend and vote, but some more populous parishes sooner or later opted for select vestries which, to a greater or lesser extent, became self-perpetuating and undemocratic bodies. At best these were seen as being more efficient and business-like; at worst they became the victims of nepotism, bribery and scandal.

The vestry appointed churchwardens, sextons and, subject to the approval of the Justices of the Peace, the overseers of the poor, the surveyors of highways, and constables or watchmen of the parish. From 1819 Croydon had a select vestry and its members were generally the wealthier residents. It would be the latter part of the 19th century before free and fair local elections were established and, even then, only householders had the vote.

The Poor Law Act of 1601 was the basis of Poor Law administration for two centuries. It divided the poor receiving relief into three categories: the able-bodied, who were to be found work; the impotent poor; and people who were unwilling to work. It required each parish to appoint annually unpaid, unskilled, often unwilling persons (usually farmers who had an interest in minimising the rate) to collect a Poor Rate and disburse it among the needy.

In 1662 the Act of Settlement was passed to try to stop people going from parish to parish in search of the most generous relief. Forty days after any person came into a parish, if they showed signs of needing relief, J.P.s were 'to remove or convey such person or persons to such parish where they were last legally settled'. Labourers looking for work had to get a settlement certificate from their own parish promising that their own overseer would take financial responsibility for them if they had to seek poor relief. Outdoor relief was given where possible, to enable people to stay in their homes; otherwise people would be sent to the workhouse. Croydon's workhouse opened at Duppas Hill in 1727.

The worst aspect of being a pauper was loss of liberty and possessions. The workhouse was seen as a 'House of Correction' and the Croydon Vestry at one time resolved that the poor in the workhouse were to have no visitors 'on any premise whatsoever'. An entry in the vestry minutes for February 1753 reads, 'Complaint being made that, several of the poor, let out of the House to hear divine service on Sabbath Days, were frequently seen about town, begging, and often drunk, it was ordered that for the future, no persons thus scandalously behaving should be suffered to go out of the House, on any pretext whatever'. Constant efforts were made to employ the poor. All those in the workhouse had to be daily employed in work and service. They worked from 6a.m. to 7p.m. in summer and from 7a.m. to 6p.m. in winter. Paupers had 'to sit at meals in a decent manner with Hands and Faces washed, Hair combed and Clothes brushed'. The old Poor Law was inconsistent in its application but profoundly adaptable. Increases in population and mobility after about 1750 led to changes in the 19th century.

Poverty was widespread. According to the Rev. Richard Baxter in 1691, poor tenants were glad of a piece of hanged bacon once a week 'enough to trie the stomach of an ostrige' and 'he is a rich man that can afford to eate a jointe of fresh meate once in a month or fortnight'. There was virtually no time for leisure activities. Wakes and feasts generally took place when farming needs were small. They were often associated with the anniversary of the dedication of the parish church. There were too a number of Christian and political holidays associated with Christmas, May Day, Guy Fawkes, Plough Monday, Shrove Tuesday and Oak Apple Day. A guide to J.P.s of 1638 stated, 'There shall be no meetings, assemblies or concourse of people for any sports or pastimes out of their own parishes on the Lord's Day, nor bear baiting, bull baiting, interludes, common playes or other unlawful exercises within their own parishes.' The definition of unlawful exercises depended on the J.P. and did not apply to the gentry! Fairs provided an occasional welcome escape from everyday drudgery. Some innkeepers provided bowling greens and billiards, and cricket is recorded as early as 1707, when a Croydon team played against London. Later in the century it seems that the local games were generally played at Duppas Hill and in 1734 'A great cricket match was lately to have been played between the Gentlemen of London and Croydon, but the latter having been regaled with a good dinner, etc, gratis, withdrew, and have since not been heard of! And the former, being desirous of playing one match before the season is expired, do challenge to play with any eleven men in England, with this exception only – that they will not admit of one from Croydon; not that they object against them as good players but as men they have an ill opinion of; having so lately had the credit of feeding the hungry they would not expose themselves to the reflections of sending the naked empty away.' Addington also had a team and claims to be one of the oldest in the country, being formed in 1743. The Croydon Bowling Club also makes a similar claim by dating its formation to 1749.

By the mid-17th century Croydon had become one of the principal towns in the county. Although of lesser importance than Guildford, Farnham or Kingston, it was the most important town in East Surrey, and during the Civil War was the administrative centre for the County Committee when it was not meeting at Kingston. In 1647 General Fairfax stayed in the town for several days and is described as having brought half his army there. In 1691, and again in 1707, Croydon applied for borough status. Approval was given on the second occasion but for some reason the decision was not implemented.

A War Office survey of 1756 recorded 781 guest beds and stabling for 359 horses in the town, substantially more than anywhere else in the county. The turnpike trusts had brought modest improvements to some of the main roads and the position of the town on a busy coaching route must have contributed to its importance. The presence of troops requiring billeting brought trade but increasing complaints from the townspeople because it caused a shortage of accommodation at market and fair times. Several petitions were submitted to the government and eventually barracks were built at Mitcham Road in 1794.

A fascinating insight into farming in the locality at the end of the 18th century is given by William Marshall in his *Minutes of Agriculture, made on a Farm of 300 acres of Various Soils, near Croydon Surry.* Published in several editions from 1778, the minutes include comments on farming methods, crops, livestock, servants and the weather. William Marshall was born in 1745 and died in 1818. He was a noted writer on agricultural matters and his works include publications on farming in Yorkshire, Gloucestershire and the Midland counties. He was a great advocate of enclosure and it is possible his writings had some influence on the movement for Croydon enclosure a few years later.

Marshall makes some general comments on the farmers of the Vale of London. They are

(the higher class excepted) as homely, in their dress and manners, as those of the more recluse parts of the Kingdom, and are far less enlightened and intelligent, than those of many parts of it. The reason is, they live chiefly among themselves, as a distinct community; retaining much of the character, probably, of husbandmen of former times; and holding their prejudices, as fast, or at this time perhaps faster, than those of the most distant provinces.

There is an excuse, however for their tenacity to established customs and practices, though not of the most eligible. They are accustomed to see ill judged plans pursued, and money wastefully expended, by the town farmers, who purchase or rent lands in their neighbourhood; and, hence, naturally enough conceive, that any

25 *(facing page)   Plan of William Marshall's farm, 1779.*

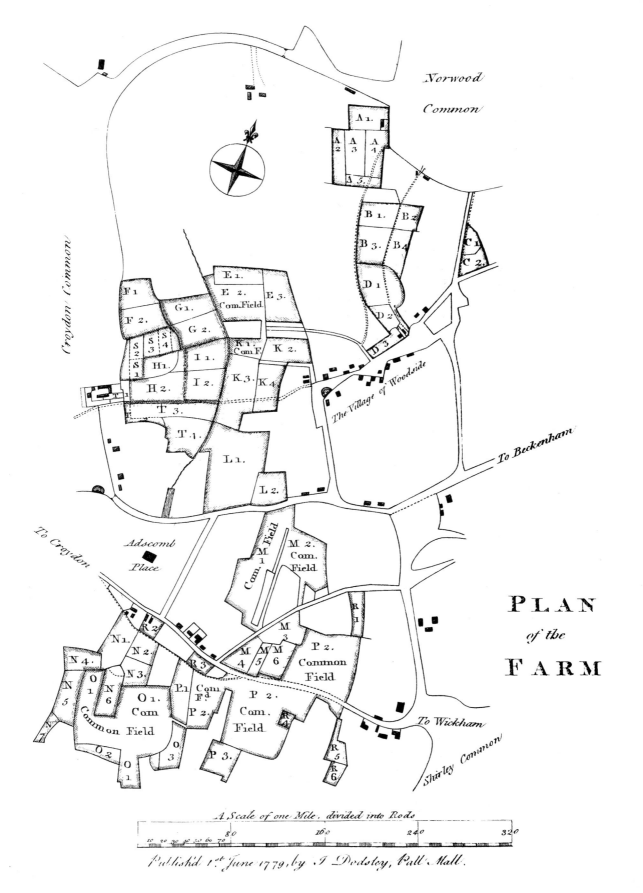

PLAN

of the

FARM

Norwood Common

Croydon Common

The Village of Woodside

To Beckenham

To Croydon

Adscomb Place

To Wickham

Shirley Common

A Scale of one Mile, divided into Rods

Publish'd 1st June 1779, by J. Dodsley, Pall Mall.

deviation from the beaten path will necessarily lead them to ruin, or involve them in a mis-carriage.

The WORK PEOPLE of the Vale wear the same marks of rusticity, as their employers. The children of farm laborers, and other poor working people, in the neighbourhood of London, rank among the most illiterate of their class, in the island. Few of them (unless of late years, through the establishment of Sunday schools) are taught, even to read.'

It is observable that at the market of Croydon, corn is sold by sample, to millers and maltsters of the neighbourhood, or to dealers who purchase for the London market.'

He describes the farm as 'situated, the most irregular and inconvenient. They had, formerly, lain in three or four distinct farms, with farm houses and offices belonging to each; three of which still remained entire: beside a detached plot, with a barn, only. The several parts lay, more or less, disjointed, by intervening property, and the different farms intermixed with other lands; parts of them being in a state of common field, parcelled out in plots of the smallest size: with the right of pasturage on two adjoining commons.

… Had I foreseen the difficulty and extent of the plan, which I have since been led to execute, I could not have fixed on a fitter subject for probation; a subject better calculated, to show the necessary variations of practice, and habituate me to the requisite versatility of management, or to call forth exertion and expedients, and inure me to the more difficult and patient employments of husbandry, than the assemblage of soils and situations, to which I was directed, by a train of fortuitous circumstances.

The HOMESTEAD, or principal Farmery, at which I resided, being placed on one side of these scattered fields, added to the difficulties of management.

The Homestead stood just a little to the north of the junction of Morland and Lower Addiscombe roads, where Morland Avenue is now. As can be seen from the plan, the farm was situated partly in Addiscombe, partly in Woodside and South Norwood, and extended as far as the common fields of Upfield and Rippingill to the south of Addiscombe Road. The only buildings remaining from the period are Addiscombe Farm and Heron's Croft in Addiscombe Road, but these were not part of his farm.

Marshall started work on this farm in 1773 and soon resolved to keep minutes, hoping that others would profit from his experiences. He soon discovered ' the unfitness of Bailiffs', so he discharged his bailiff, who he suspected of smuggling, and took over the farm himself. The following extracts from the minutes tell us something of farming conditions in Croydon 230 years ago:

3rd February 1775 Harnessed the oxen, in all their new finery; – their fringes and tassels; – their gaudy bridles and housings. The Pantheon never saw more ridiculous macaronies. But what is still more ridiculous, the very men, who fancied it beneath them to associate with oxen, are now ambitious of being the companions of HORNED HORSES! and their new name, and finery, have had the desired effect.

In the field they behaved very well; but coming into the yard, one of them broke loose, with his trappings upon him, and put the pigs and poultry in bodily fear; – a bated bull was never more furious; and it is well that it ended in fear.

4th Got a nose ring made, for the riotous ox.

Oxen seem to have been commonly used on the wet clay lands in the late 18th and early 19th centuries.

Working on Sundays was very much disapproved of, but Marshall was prepared to ignore the opinion of others if he thought it necessary:

8th October 1775 I lost one fine Sunday this year, and took a lesson from the folly. After dinner got the teams to work and carried all Foot-path-Field in very good order.

I hope no harm is done – not even to religion; for I fancy that I see his Grace of Canterbury's team carrying him, perhaps from a vicious scene of luxurious guttling. It now rains!

I have given the labourers, who were all very ready to help, a Sunday's dinner, and some ale in the evening; but sent them home sober

26 *This print dated 1785 is called* View on the Footroad to Croydon. *The stream in the foreground indicates that it could depict the Norbury area where the River Graveney is of about the width shown.*

to their wives and children. Farmer ****** made his men so intolerably drunk the other night that one of them was suffocated by the liquor; leaving a widow and four children to be kept by the parish. Such is the effect of Harvest-Suppers!

14th November 1775 TWO-WHEEL WAGGON. Took a pair of iron-arms and six-inch from a dung-cart, and put them under the Handy. I may be vain, but I am clearly of opinion, that a more perfect Farmer's carriage for a level country cannot be conceived. She hugs a load-and-a-half of straw, or a load of hay, cleverly; and with the iron-arms, runs much lighter than a waggon.

I have put-by the waggons till next hay-time; for their narrow wheels are ill adapted to Croydon Common in winter.

She is a most eligible dung-cart, and will carry as much chaff, cavil, etc as two or three of the common ones.

2nd February 1776 ... On Sunday 7th, there was a storm of rain and snow, and on Monday morning, a deep snow.

From that time until yesterday (three weeks and four days), we have had very severe weather. The snow falling remarkably dry, with a high wind, it was very much drifted; in some places,

six or eight feet deep; and the crowns of high ridges were left entirely bare.

6th June 1776 IN-DOOR SERVANTS – PRICE OF PROVISIONS

On the maturest calculation, I make the yearly expence of a man in the house £35 and of a boy, £23. (Supposing the man's wages to be £10 and the boy's £3 a year.)

The yearly expence of a day-labouring man (if he works every day) is but £27 10s. 0d. And that of a boy, but £13. 0s. 0d.

The difference therefore between keeping a man in the house, and hiring one by the day, is, beside rainy days, £7 10s. 0d. And the difference between a boy in the house and one by the day is £10. 0s. 0d. More than 3-4ths of a day-boy's wages!

The impropriety therefore of keeping plow-boys in the house, is clearly proved; and tho' it may be convenient to have the Carters about home; I think that conveniency is not worth £7 10s. 0d. a year: I will therefore put a woman into the cottage (within two hundred paces of the Farm-yard) to take in lodgers; and I am determined not to have, in future, more farming-servants in the house than a Bustler and a Yard-man.

It is absolutely necessary to have somebody in a Farm-yard, in case of emergency; and I

think these will be sufficient: for the Carters in the cottage will be nearly as handy, as if they were in the house.

Perhaps the Farmer who keeps no accounts imagines he saves money by boarding his servants in the house: but I am confident, that if he keeps them in that luxurious style which farming-servants in this country expect to be kept in, he is quite mistaken.

Were I to reason POLITICALLY, it would be thus: Farming-servants form a large part of the community. Perhaps, one in the house, one fed by his master, costs the community as much as two who provide for themselves: for discharge a grumbler, one who pretends to be dissatisfied, tho' in fact satiated, and he will return to his bread-and-cheese with, perhaps, equal health and equal happiness. He sits down to his master's table with a resolution to eat voraciously of the best, to do himself justice; but, at his own, eats sparingly of the meanest, to save his money. His motive, in both cases, is the same: Self-interest!

Therefore, feeding farming-servants in the house lessens the quantity, and of course enhances the price of provisions.

27 (facing page)   The Commissioners appointed by the Enclosure Act prepared a plan and award which described the various roads and footpaths within the parish. Many of these already existed and were ancient highways. Some may well have been ill-defined tracks. The parcels of land were numbered and listed so that they could be allocated to their recipients. The names of the owners of some of the land are shown.

Many of the fields already existed and their names are very descriptive. The map on the opposite page has the town centre in the middle. To the left is Waddon Marsh Lane, now largely replaced by Purley Way. Mitcham Road ran from near top left past the barracks to Pitlake and Church Street. Broad Green is top centre with Handcroft Road running south. London Road, North End, High Street and South End ran from top centre to bottom centre. The turnpike gate is shown adjacent to Turnpike Field, just north of the Brighton Road / Selsdon Road junction.

Old Town ran south from Church Street into Southbridge Road, with Lower Coombe Street leading to Coombe Road towards the east. Note that a small enclosure (1311) is named Hop Garden; hops are known to have been grown locally at one time. Note also the nearby Chalk Pit (1401) and Brick Kiln Mead (1407).

Fairfield Path ran across Fair Field towards Coombe. Much of it still exists. George Street and Addiscombe Road (centre right) led eastwards from the town centre, with Park Lane running south to Coombe Road, and Wellesley Road leading north across St James's Road to Whitehorse Road, which was linked to Broad Green by Windmill Road, the windmill being shown. The present names have been used in this description. Some of the roads already bore their current names but others did not.

21st August 1776 – BUSTLING I never made a better day's work than I have done to-day. How? Thro' the means of omnipotent bribery.

Last night, after a hard day's work, I gave the men as much ale as they would drink: This morning, after they had unloaded the waggons, I gave them two gallons to their breakfasts; which I desired them to eat while the horses were feeding. The teams were presently sent out; the men went singing into the field; and, working like coal-heavers, never looked behind them, until we had made up a stack of about twenty loads: It was run up in about five hours!

I now repeated the dose; and in the afternoon we gathered up as many odds-and-ends, as, without the ale, would have amounted to a day's work.

This evening I have been canvassing for a great day's work tomorrow.

2nd September 1776 The harvest-month ended last Saturday the 1st. (It is an established custom here, for every man, in harvest, to work by the acre, or by the month; not by the day. If a labourer be employed constantly thro' the year, he expects, during harvest, to be constantly employed on mowing, reaping, etc. by the acre, or to have his harvest-month; that is, to have an advance of wages, certain, wet or dry, during one month; which month commences when it best suits his employer.)

I had this year, seven month-men and two boys; and two men in the house: in all, nine men, and two boys, by the month or year. But I was two or three men short. Ten men, two boys, and three teams are all sett for carrying, if the distance be less than half-a-mile; if more, four teams, and of course eleven men are necessary.

Month-men are very convenient; they are always at command, in cases of emergency; and nothing but a continuance of rain while the barns are empty, can make them burdensome. And in future I will endeavour to have not less than twelve men by the month, or year. The ox-team, this year, was sometimes obliged to lie-by for want of a Plowman; and a Plow-team in August is invaluable.

9th September 1776 HUNTING Last week, Mr. ******'s hounds came across the standing-corn. I desired that they might be kept off the Farm, until the corn be off the ground.

This morning Mr. ******'s huntsman and whipper-in were absolutely trailing in and around a field of beans and buck-wheat, with a field of barley in swath adjoining. I ordered them off; but they presently returned, and I was under the necessity of sending them away in a much greater hurry the second time than the first …

10th October 1776 SERVANTS Reduced my in-door Farming-servants to two; a Bustler and a Yard-boy. (Since October 1775) till now, I have had a young fellow, a Farmer's son, in the house; but I have been again out of luck: Poor Richard has no Devil in him; and a Bustler without spirit is not worth a straw.

From Methodism he flew to love, and from love to the Quack Doctor. Fools are ever prey to the designing. No sooner did I rescue him from the fangs of one, than another seized him; and with difficulty I have returned him to his father, not more indolent nor foolish than I received him.

3rd March 1777 … About two years ago, I took a lad, who was puny and unfit for hard labour, from the plow, and placed him in the house. The first year he behaved very well; the second, tolerably; but a falling off was obvious. His brother, the preceding year, had suffered much for want of correction, and I clearly saw that he was striding away apace to the same path. I therefore, though reluctantly, began to administer the necessary discipline; and during that year it had the desired effect.

His vice commenced with idle excuses; from these he crept on to falsehood; and perhaps, this may be held as a general maxim: The first step to destruction is evasion; the second, lying; the third, pilfering; thieving, murder, and the gallows, follow of course: cunning or impertinence is generally an accomplice.

This, the third year, he has behaved very ill. I was aware of evil Counsellors, but could not identify them. At length the horsewhip totally lost its efficacy; and I, tired of correcting, sent to his friends: but he in the meantime (by the advice of his Council) went to a Magistrate, under the pretence of recovering his liberty and wages.

The Magistrate, whose head is as good as his heart is honest, presently saw thro' the rascality, and sent him home; and generously assisted his friends in discovering the incendiaries. Astonishing! one of them, a man who has worked for me upwards of two years, and whom I have, lately, been endeavouring to serve; the other (the principal), a fellow whom I have employed near twelve months, and who, in the height of his tutorship, fetched his son out of a distant county, to enjoy from me the advantages of constant employment and good usage! Nor is the boy, though he promises implicit obedience in future, free from guilt; for if the advice had not been palatable, he would not have swallowed it so greedily; and him I have been particularly assiduous to serve: I have not only taken upon myself the disagreeable task of beating him, but have rendered him other benefits which must last him his life. And I am under the most disagreeable necessity of drawing an inference, which must inevitably deprive me, in future, of a very great satisfaction; and I will not smother my sentiments, when I believe that they were kindled by truth; and I am at present clearly of opinion, that GOOD USAGE MAKES BAD SERVANTS; I speak generally; and by good usage, I mean extraordinarily good usage.

28 (facing page) This part of the enclosure map covers much of the eastern part of the parish. Woodside is near top right, with Blackhorse Lane leading south to Lower Addiscombe Road and Long Lane running across from left to right. The Homestead in which William Marshall lived is between numbers 698 and 700 to the left of the plan. Addiscombe House is clearly shown and Addiscombe Road runs to the south, then north of Upfield.

The road (centre right) leading from Barn Field (1206) to Shirley Road (856) disappeared in the 20th century. It rejoiced in the name of Slutts Hall Lane. It will be noted that Addiscombe Road curved to the south as it passed Upfield and continued into Wickham Road. The road divided land belonging to John Claxton of Shirley House (later Shirley Park Hotel and now the site of the Trinity School of John Whitgift). Apparently, some years after enclosure Colonel Maberley, the new owner, was unhappy about the road passing so close to his house. He managed to get it diverted by inviting numerous local dignitaries and magistrates to dinner then blocking the road with farm waggons so as to make it difficult for the guests to get to his house! Present day traffic congestion is no doubt worse as an indirect result of this dinner party!

Towards the bottom of the map, Coombe Road led south-east to the parish boundary at Coombe. Conduit Lane ran between 1275 and 1274. A short section of the present Oaks Road led to 1236, while Oaks Lane led direct from Coombe Road across Oaks Farm towards Shirley. The Chalk Pit (1253) still exists, although long disused.

Common 641

514
726 Hen.ᵉ Smale 727
725
724
723
Rays Fᵈ 728
J.Humphreys
729 Croydon Hospital
730
731
732
722 721 720
W. S. Watton
Laylands
A. Adair Esq.

509
755
761
771
770
Josh Humphrey 756
Cooks Mead
R. Woodyer 754
Free Mead
760
772 773
Josh Humphrey 774
Alderman Field
810
809
Home Field 814
824
J. Har
757
758
G. Bailey
759
Alice Sims 752
753
751 Croydon Hospital
749
Ann Marden
Woodside Green
776
J. Brookes 776
Admirals Mead
777
Woods Mead 778
Richd Woodyer
805
806
808 807
804
803
802
Pam Mead
801
800
R. Woodyer 793
792
Willets Field
Jos.
Hardy

644
645
646
648
649
650 651
652
653
716
717
712 713
6. 99
711 710
700
698
705 706
697
701 704
696 703
691 692 693
695

719
714
708
734
735
Croydon Hospital
748
747
746
750
781
760
Small Profits 736
Mid Fᵈ 745
743 H.
744 Smale
742
741
R. Woodyer
737 J. Hardy
740 Mary Lewen
739
738
779 Richd Woodyer Barn Field
782
785 Geo. Bailey
783 784
786
Josh Humphrey Esq.
851
853
850
852
854 Stroud Green
Croydon Hospital
1150
1153
1152
1149
848
Croydon
847
845
846 Croydon Hospital
845

1455
1461 1463
1454
1459
1457 1460
1455 1456
ickwood Esq.
1464

Meadow 1179
Meadow 1178
1177 8 Acres Mead
1176 Canal Mead
1175
1174 1173
1180
Cha.ˢ Jn.ᵒ Clarke Esq.
Great Mead
Lower Mead
ADDISCOMBE
Addiscombe Place 1172
Wilderness
1170 Upper Mead
1171
1154
1168
1169 Great Mead
1167
1162
A. Adair Esq.
1164
1156
Clays 1155
1157 Little Clays Alex. Adair Esq.
1158
1161
1163
999 Apple Haugh
998 Pasmore Haugh
997
996 New Leys
1000
1165
1166
Croydon Hospital 995
Fingats Fields 1146
1147 Jnᵒ Brookes Esq.
1145
855
1001 1002 1003
A. Adair
859 Croydon Hospital
857 858
860 861
862
863
864 865
Alex.ʳ Adair Esq.
867
868
870 Croydon Hospital 871
869
Croydon Hospital 992
993
J. Cooper
985
930
982
New 963 Fᵈ
986 987
988
989
981 980
J. Claxton Esq.
1220 981
978
Jnᵒ Claxton Esq.
1218
1225
977
1226
Peartree 923
924
Robbers Hole
Lit. Hill 926 Field
Long 925 Mead
936 Brook Haws
928
Cow Pasture 930
Brookly
922
Grove
87
Hospi
Alex.ʳ Adair Esq.
Jnᵒ Cla

1419 Smiths 7 Acres
op 1420
ry
1421
1413
Pond d
1412
1181 Park Field
Croydon Hospital 1182
1184 Home Field
1183 Scrubbs
1185
1186
1204
1187 North New Croft
1188 South New Croft
Little Crabtree 1417 Close
Gᵗ Crabtree 1416 Close
Long 1192 6 Acres
1190 1189
Conduit Field
1197
1198 Alex. Adair
Croydon Hospital 1191
T. Meager Senᵗ 1196
Rippingill
1193
Squashes 1031
1165
1202 Alex.ʳ Adair
1208 Alex.ʳ Adair
1203
Barn 1206 Field
1205
UPFIELD
1212
1209 Croydon Hospital
A. Adair 1210 Fowleaze
Croydon Hospital 1211
1214
1215
1216
1219 Brick Close
1221
1217
Wards 1229 Field
1247 Brakey Close
976
1228
1231
1214
1213 Barn Field
933 Fiel
Barn
925

Great Chalk 1411 Hill
halk
1415
1193
C. J. Clarke Esq. 1194
Squashes 1303
Hammonds 1300 Hill
L. Field
1305
Great New 1304 Field
Little New 1295 Field
1296 James Bourdieu Esq.
Spoake
1258 Bourdieu Esq. Fields
1255 Barn
1253 Chalk Pit
1254
1242
1243
1250
Bateson's 1249 Hill
Bishops 1248 Field
1246
1230 Breoks
975
972
Jnᵒ Aa
Co

1306 Pyes Field
Pit 1307 Croft
J. Bourdieu 1309
Lower Pit 1308 Field
1313
131 4
1219
Pit Field 1290
1292 Vineyard Field
1293 Paddock
1265
1297 Wood
1299 1298
1300
Kitchen Field 1257
1256
Volcians 1251
Ricketts Hill 1252
1241
1238
1260 Paddock
1264
1262
1267
1268
1237
1239
Oaks Farm 1240
1244 1245
The Archbishop of Canterbury
1235
1234
1233
1232
1274
COOMBE

1316
1317
spital
Scrubbs 1288
Adams 1281
1280
1277
1266 1276
1277
1275
1273
1269 1272
1236
Summer 1270 House Field
J. Bourdieu Esq. Senᵗ Conduit

29 *This 2001 view shows a ploughing bank in Lloyd Park, looking south from approximately where the narrow strip (1291 on the Enclosure Map, previous page, bottom left) meets Great New Field (1304). Such features occur after many years of ploughing leaves a large bank at the edge of a field In this area they could be made larger by flints being dragged to the edge of a field.*

Enclosure of the Common Lands

The advantages of enclosed and compact farms under one man's control had been widely appreciated for several centuries. The common-field system was wasteful, expensive and difficult to work so long as dispersed holdings, common grazing rights and sharing of the commons remained its basis.

Gradual enclosure and exchange of strips had taken place on a small scale for a long time but the process of parliamentary enclosure got under way in about 1760. It meant a rapid addition to the land under cultivation of large tracts of commons and waste, and for the common fields a speedy conversion to the conditions necessary for more efficient farming. Enclosure was generally profitable to landlords and farmers alike. During the French wars a great deal of the enclosure activity was concerned

with bringing marginal lands into production.

In 1796 some of the leading local landowners in Croydon petitioned Parliament for leave to introduce a Private Bill, and this passed through all its stages in a couple of months. There was some opposition from the poor of Croydon petitioning against the loss of their common rights, which included the grazing of sheep, cows and horses and gathering underwood for fuel. The Act, probably as a sop to the petitioners, included provision for at least 215 acres to be retained as open common. In the event the Enclosure Commissioners allowed 237 acres to remain unenclosed, out of the 2,950 acres of common lands within the parish before the passing of the Act in 1797, but the 237 acres were not to last very long. The Trustees appointed to administer them were the vicar, the churchwardens, the overseers of the poor, and six appointees of the vestry. In 1806 they decided that 237 acres in 28 different pieces were of little use to the parishioners and should be sold to pay for the building of a new Town Hall and Butter Market, and an additional burial ground. A further Act was obtained to allow this to be done and Croydon's commons disappeared for ever.

There is little doubt that before enclosure the cottager was a labourer with land, but after enclosure he was a labourer without land. In Croydon, enclosure gave the common lands to a number of landowners who, in the following decades, would be able to make far more profitable use out of their property than by farming it. Transport improvements and the close proximity of the parish to London would see it transformed by building development. The growing town would have to pay large sums to buy back even small areas to provide open spaces and parks for the enjoyment of the parishioners.

V

Growing Pains 1801-1851

THE YEAR 1801 saw the first modern census, with Croydon recording 5,743 inhabitants. Apart from the town centre there was a scattering of houses along the London Road and small settlements existed at Waddon, Thornton Heath near the pond, at Broad Green and at Woodside. A few gentlemen's residences had appeared on the Norwood Hills and there were some country estates such as those at Addiscombe and at Coombe. Some better-off people had moved to the area from London and in the early 19th century William Cobbett described Croydon as '… a good market town but swelled by the funds into a wen'.

Transport Improvements

Transport was entirely by horse and road surfaces were generally poor, even where the Turnpike Trusts had effected improvements. Pack horses carried many of the smaller goods and large wagons often got bogged down in the muddy roads. Regular stage-coach services connected the town with London, Brighton and a few other places.

In 1799 a group of Wandle Valley industrialists had proposed a canal up the valley, but concern over abstraction of water from the river and its effect on the many water-powered mills led instead to the adoption of a scheme for an iron railway. There were already a number of railways or plateways, mainly in the north of England and Wales. Some were of wood, some iron, and all were privately-owned; they were horse-drawn and served mines, factories, quarries and canals. In 1801 the Surrey Iron Railway (SIR) was the first public railway to be authorised by Parliament. It linked Wandsworth and Croydon, with a branch from Mitcham to Hackbridge, and was formally opened on 26 July 1803.

At the end of the 18th and beginning of the 19th centuries England was at war with France. There was a general desire for an improved inland link between London and the country's main naval port of Portsmouth because of the danger to shipping in the English Channel. The engineer to the SIR, William Jessop, had foreseen in his original report that the line might form the first part of a link to Portsmouth and this was very much in mind when an extension of the railway was planned to the chalk quarries at Merstham. The Croydon, Merstham and Godstone Iron Railway (CMGIR), seen as the first stage, received its Act of Parliament in May 1803 and was formally opened to Merstham on 24 July 1805. In fact it never reached Godstone. Both railways had cast-iron, 'L'-shaped rails laid on stone blocks. The wheels of the wagons had flat treads; they were owned by the users, who had to pay tolls for use of the line.

At the same time as the plans for the SIR were being developed, separate promoters were planning a canal from Deptford to Croydon. Their Act received Royal Assent in 1801, only a few weeks after the SIR, but it was not until 1809 that the canal was fully open. Again the promoters hoped to extend it to Portsmouth. The canal needed 26 locks to raise it from the Grand Surrey Canal at Deptford to Forest Hill, with two more locks at Selhurst. The canal company laid a short railway

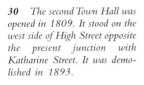
30 The second Town Hall was opened in 1809. It stood on the west side of High Street opposite the present junction with Katharine Street. It was demolished in 1893.

line from its wharf at West Croydon to link up with the SIR and CMGIR at Pitlake. This seems to have adversely affected trade on the SIR and much of its traffic was diverted to the canal. Croydon had become the first town in the country to be connected by a public railway and a canal, but it seems there was insufficient traffic to justify the two modes and both suffered as a result. The trade on both railways and the canal was principally coals, fir timber, groceries, stone, slate, malt and manure upwards from London, and downwards from Croydon it was oak, elm timber, firestone, lime, fuller's earth, flints, flour and seeds. As it passed through some very attractive countryside the canal soon became a leisure attraction and was popular with anglers, with skaters in winter and for outings by boat. The *Dartmouth Arms* (Forest Hill), the *Greyhound* (Sydenham) and the *Jolly Sailor* (Norwood) had popular tea gardens.

By the 1830s steam railways had developed and the canal suffered problems with leaks and collapsed banks. In 1834 the London and Croydon Railway Company was set up and it bought the canal and closed it in 1836. Parts of the alignment were used

by the railway company but quite a few short sections remained for many years. South Norwood Lake, which was originally larger, was the main reservoir, and still provides angling and sailing facilities. The two early railways operated for only a few more years. The CMGIR was bought and closed in 1838 by the London and Brighton Railway, which needed part of its route. The SIR struggled on until 1846, when it too succumbed. Tamworth Road was laid out on the alignment of the canal company's line, and Church Road is the former alignment of the CMGIR through the town centre.

In the mid-1830s Parliament had apparently decided there should be only one railway route out of London to the south. The London and Croydon Railway therefore had to run over the Greenwich Railway (opened from 1836) from London Bridge, leaving it at Corbett's Lane north of New Cross. The London and Brighton Railway then had to run over both to Selhurst, where it started its own line, and the South Eastern Railway (to Dover) had to run over all three and then branch off at Redhill. Each company had to pay tolls to the companies over whose lines it ran. Between East Croydon and

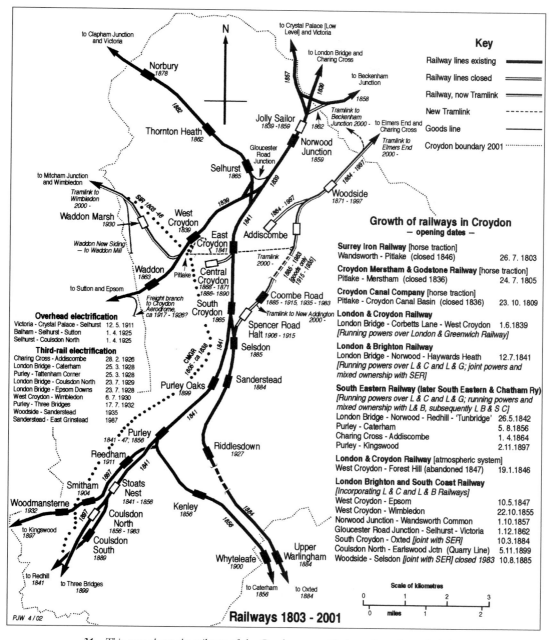

to Clapham Junction
and Victoria

to Crystal Palace [Low
Level] and Victoria

N

to London Bridge and
Charing Cross

Key

Railway lines existing

Railway lines closed

Railway, now Tramlink

New Tramlink

Goods line

Croydon boundary 2001

Norbury
1878

1882

to Beckenham
Junction

1858

Thornton Heath
1862

Jolly Sailor
1839 -1859   1862

Tramlink to
Beckenham
Junction 2000 -

to Elmers End and
Charing Cross

Gloucester
Road
Junction

Norwood
Junction
1859

Tramlink to
Elmers End
2000 -

Selhurst
1865

1839

to Mitcham Junction
and Wimbledon

Tramlink to
Wimbledon
2000 -

SVR 1926-48

1839

Woodside
1871 - 1997

1884 - 1997

Waddon Marsh
1930

West
Croydon
1839

East
Croydon
1841

Addiscombe

1884 - 1997

Growth of railways in Croydon
— opening dates —

Waddon New Siding
– to Waddon Mill

Tramlink
2000 -

Surrey Iron Railway [horse traction]
Wandsworth - Pitlake (closed 1846)   26. 7. 1803

Waddon
1863   Pitlake

Central
Croydon
1868 - 1871
1886- 1890

1886 - 1883
goods only
1915 - 1935

Croydon Merstham & Godstone Railway [horse traction]
Pitlake - Merstham (closed 1836)   24. 7. 1805

to Sutton and Epsom

Coombe Road
1885 - 1915, 1935 - 1983

Croydon Canal Company [horse traction]
Pitlake - Croydon Canal Basin (closed 1836)   23. 10. 1809

Freight branch
to Croydon
Aerodrome,
ca 1917 - 1926?

South
Croydon
1865

Tramlink to New Addington
2000 -

London & Croydon Railway
London Bridge - Corbetts Lane - West Croydon   1.6.1839
[Running powers over London & Greenwich Railway]

Overhead electrification
Victoria - Crystal Palace - Selhurst   12. 5. 1911
Balham - Selhurst - Sutton   1. 4. 1925
Selhurst - Coulsdon North   1. 4. 1925

Spencer Road
Halt 1906 - 1915

Selsdon
1885

London & Brighton Railway
London Bridge - Norwood - Haywards Heath   12.7.1841
[Running powers over L & C and L & G; joint powers and
mixed ownership with SER]

Third-rail electrification
Charing Cross - Addiscombe   28. 2. 1926
London Bridge - Caterham   25. 3. 1928
Purley - Tattenham Corner   25. 3. 1928
London Bridge - Coulsdon North   23. 7. 1929
London Bridge - Epsom Downs   23. 7. 1928
West Croydon - Wimbledon   6. 7. 1930
Purley - Three Bridges   17. 7. 1932
Woodside - Sanderstead   1935
Sanderstead - East Grinstead   1987

Sanderstead
1884

CMGR 1805

1856 ca 1839

1841

South Eastern Railway (later South Eastern & Chatham Ry)
[Running powers over L & C and L & G; running powers and
mixed ownership with L & B, subsequently L B & S C]
London Bridge - Norwood - Redhill - 'Tunbridge'   26.5.1842
Purley - Caterham   5. 8.1856
Charing Cross - Addiscombe   1. 4.1864
Purley - Kingswood   2.11.1897

Purley Oaks
1899

1841

London & Croydon Railway [atmospheric system]
West Croydon - Forest Hill (abandoned 1847)   19.1.1846

Purley
1841 - 47; 1856

Riddlesdown
1927

London Brighton and South Coast Railway
[Incorporating L & C and L & B Railways]
West Croydon - Epsom   10.5.1847
West Croydon - Wimbledon   22.10.1855
Norwood Junction - Wandsworth Common   1.10.1857
Gloucester Road Junction - Selhurst - Victoria   1.12.1862
South Croydon - Oxted [joint with SER]   10.3.1884
Coulsdon North - Earlswood Jctn (Quarry Line)   5.11.1899
Woodside - Selsdon [joint with SER] closed 1983   10.8.1885

Reedham
1911

1897

Smitham
1904

Stoats
Nest
1841 - 1856

Kenley
1856

1854

Woodmansterne
1932

1897

Coulsdon
North
1856 - 1983

1856

to Kingswood
1897

Coulsdon
South
1889

Upper
Warlingham
1884

to Redhill
1841

to Three Bridges
1899

Whyteleafe
1900

to Caterham
1856

to Oxted
1884

Scale of kilometres
0   1   2   3
0   miles   1   2

PJW 4 / 02

Railways 1803 - 2001

31   This map shows the railways of the Croydon area, with dates of opening and closing.

Redhill the line north of Stoat's Nest was owned by the Brighton company, and south to Redhill by the South Eastern Company. These complicated arrangements have caused many problems over the years both to the companies and to passengers.

By 1841 the town had two railway stations (the present East and West) as well as one at Norwood named after the local hostelry, the *Jolly Sailor*. Then in 1847 a line from West Croydon to Epsom was opened. The previous year had seen an experiment with atmospheric traction on the London and Croydon Railway but the project was abandoned. The Croydon and Brighton railways merged in 1846 to form the London, Brighton and South Coast Railway.

Croydon in 1818

A contemporary account of the town in the early 19th century is given by the Rev D.W. Garrow in the *History of Croydon* published in 1818:

> The town consists chiefly of one well-built street, near a mile in length; called the High Street … Here are situated the Court house, the two Markets, with excellent shops and inns – the shops plentifully supplied with the various

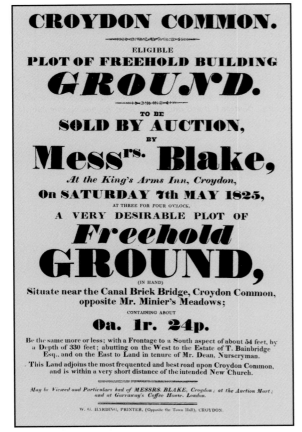

32 This 1825 poster advertising land for building purposes confirms that Croydon's popularity as a residential area was growing by this time.

articles necessary in the different branches of trade, administer materially to the convenience and comfort of the numerous families in the town and its vicinity. At the principal Inns travellers experience the most assiduous attention and best accommodation, both during the time of their continuance, and also respecting their further progress on the road … [Since the 1811 census] there has been a further increase of houses to about 1,540, in which is included the Workhouse, which contains 160 people – therefore, taking the whole together in the proportion of 6½ to each house, which taking the Workhouse and Barracks at the same ratio, will make the number of inhabitants 10,010, we may consider the present population of Croydon, as amounting to nearly 10,000 souls.

Three years later the 1821 census recorded the population as 9,254.

Garrow then describes the rating districts:

> East side of High-street Which begins at the George corner, takes all the East side of the street, includes the Mint Walk, Spotted Dog Yard, Bailey's Yard, Teg's Court, Coombe Lane, Boswell Court, and Haling; and contains about 180 houses:

> West side of High-street Takes all the West side from Crown hill to Haling, including the Anchor, back lane, Green Dragon, and Scarbrook; comprising about 170 houses:

> The Three Tuns Takes the place of that name, the Butcher Row, Spring Walk, with Benson's, and Dog and Bull Yards; comprising about 90 houses:

> The Middle-street with Huson's court etc contains about 65 Houses

> Pitlake, the lower part of the town so called, with the Barracks, the Road and Railway 60 Houses

> Lower and upper Church-street, with the Palace, a Court and Hand-croft Alley 112 Houses

> The Old Town and Ridley's Rents 110 Houses

> Duppa's Hill and Little London 30 Houses

> Waddon and Waddon Lane 35 Houses

> North End, with Webb's and Stone Mason's yards 85 Houses

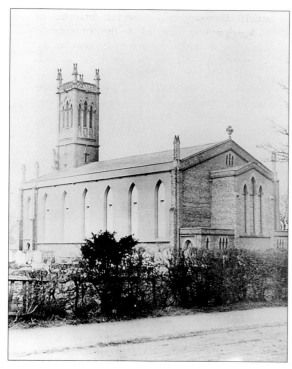

33   St James's Church, Croydon Common was opened in 1829 to serve a new parish for the increasing population in that part of the town. This photograph shows the church in 1863. It was subsequently enlarged but closed in 1980 and has since been converted into residential accommodation.

34   The second new parish to be established in 1829 was All Saints', Norwood. It was intended to serve the growing population on the Norwood heights.

Broad Green and Bencham-lane 85 Houses

Thornton Heath 65 Houses

Norwood and Blind Corner 160 Houses

The Common 135 Houses

Wood-side, Addiscombe, and Shirley 85 Houses

Coombe, Croham, and Selsdon 30 Houses

Back-Lane, Newgate, and George-street 50 Houses

Garrow then describes the Court House and Butter Market and continues by discussing trade:

But since, by means of good turnpike roads, the Canal, and the Railway, a better communication has been made through Croydon, between the interior of the County and the Metropolis, the country has been opened to trade; and men of industry, perseverance, and property have embarked as merchants in a general course of business. They take off the produce of the Country, such as corn, seeds, hops, etc. and in return, supply both the town and neighbourhood with such articles as are principally required. Through their assiduity the Corn-markets have very much increased within the last few years; and here perhaps is the best market on the Southern side of London. In Croydon are excellent shops of every description: and the different handicrafts necessary or appertaining to trade are carried on in various parts of the town. A lace manufactory conducted by machinery was established at the palace, but is now discontinued. Here are also bleaching grounds, for calicos and cottons, which serve also for the purpose of drying them after the operation of printing.

He then describes the theatre as 'open five or six weeks during the months of October and November', and continues with Assemblies:

At Croydon, are two very spacious and convenient rooms for this purpose, having orchestras and proper accommodation for the band. One of these rooms is at the King's Arms inn, and the other at the Grey-hound, where the gentry of the town, and its vicinity, have a monthly ball, with cards for the amusement of those who may not be disposed to join the dance. The expenses are defrayed by subscription, and the assemblies are held on the Monday after every full moon.

Billiards were available

For the amusement of gentlemen, who may be inclined occasionally to pass an hour at this pleasing game, Mr Boon, at the Grey-hound has fitted up a room, and provided a very good table at great expense. The terms are, for each game, in the day time 3d. at night 6d. on account of fire and candles.

Garrow also mentions the facilities for hunting, the barracks, the Dissenters' chapels, and the Book Society:

This like many others in different parts of the country, is an association for the desirable purpose of affording to many respectable and well-informed persons, who may not have the means of procuring the numerous publications of the present day, the opportunity of perusing instructive and entertaining books. According to the rules of the society, every member pays £2 2s. per annum, as a contribution, for the purchase of such books as the society may approve; which of course every subscriber is entitled to read, but necessarily for a limited time. At the expiration of every year. there is a meeting of the society, at the King's Arms, when the books are disposed of amongst the members, to each highest bidder.

The Book Society continued in existence at the rebuilt *King's Arms* until 1953.

The Improvement Commissioners

Croydon may have entered a period of declining trade by the 1820s. The anonymous author of a pamphlet published in 1829 blamed the archbishops for neglecting the town because they had treated it

as a place of refuge and not as a place of business. The author was, one suspects, a local businessman with an axe to grind as he recommended amongst other things frequent markets and fairs to attract people to the town, with a new market place, a gaol and new roads.

In fact, by the 1820s it had become apparent that the select vestry was not capable of dealing with all the problems of a growing town. In 1829 an Act for lighting, watching and improving the Town of Croydon in the County of Surrey set up the Improvement Commissioners. They had responsibility also for preventing cock-fighting, dog-fighting and bull-baiting in the streets, and for providing a place of confinement for prisoners.

A fire service of sorts had been provided since 1745 and a gas works was established in 1829. There were parish constables and watchmen but otherwise the locality relied on the Bow Street foot and horse patrols. It was expected that a police force would soon be established for the metropolis, that this would include Croydon, and that it might be a considerable burden on the local rates. A local police force was therefore set up in an attempt to keep the Metropolitan Police out of the town. At the end of 1829 Richard Coleman, a former Bow Street Runner, was appointed Sergeant and he and three privates took the oath. The men had uniforms of blue pantaloons, blue coat and red waistcoat. They were armed with pistol and cutlass. When sober Coleman was an energetic law officer, but he and others in the force were frequently unable to carry out their duties because they were drunk. In 1833 Coleman had pawned his pistols and missed the Assizes which all the police were required to attend. After being removed from the fair in 1838 in a state of intoxication, he resigned from the force.

The police were not very popular and complaints were made about their conduct on numerous occasions. As time elapsed the strength of the force increased. At first they patrolled only during the hours of darkness, but continual complaints about idle and dissolute boys creating a disturbance by congregating near the Butter Market in the High

Street, and of a vast influx of beggars and vagrants, led to patrols being on duty during the day from 1836. The local force had a short life but a merry one. Just as it was becoming a little more efficient and reasonably well organised, the Metropolitan Police were introduced into Croydon and neighbouring parishes. In 1840 the Croydon Police were disbanded, and within a few weeks the Clerk to the Improvement Commissioners was instructed to write to the Metropolitan Commissioner complaining of an insufficiency of police in the area of the common, of loose and disorderly women in the town, and of juvenile thieves!

Paupers, Hunters and Gypsies

In 1834 the Poor Law Amendment Act established Poor Law Unions to bring together a number of parishes. Croydon Union was set up in 1836 under a Board of Guardians. It comprised the parishes of Croydon, Addington, Coulsdon, Sanderstead, Woodmansterne, Beddington with Wallington, Mitcham, Merton, Morden and Penge (which was at that time in Surrey as a detached portion of Battersea parish). The Croydon Workhouse had been built in 1727 on Duppas Hill and had to be enlarged to cope with the greater area now covered. Conditions

35   This statue of Robert Surtees' character, Mr Jorrocks, shows him in a characteristic position. It stands in George Street adjacent to St Matthew's House and was photographed in November 2001. One of Croydon's new trams is reflected in the window.

in workhouses varied considerably but often most of the inhabitants were the aged, poor, and young children. Males, females and families were usually separated, and there was a justified dread of 'being sent to the workhouse' which survived well into the 20th century.

Croydon was well known as a centre for fox-hunting and field sports in general. The Duke of

36   A gypsy encampment at Woodside about 1890. In the background is the railway line between Woodside and Addiscombe, with the Dalmally Passage bridge behind the tent.

Grafton is recorded as having kept a pack of fox-hounds at Croydon in 1735. The 19th-century writer, Robert Smith Surtees, caricatured Surrey hunting in *Jorrocks' Jaunts and Jollities* in 1838: 'The town of Croydon, nine miles from the standard in Cornhill, is the general rendezvous of the gallant sportsmen. It is the principal market-town in the eastern division of the county of Surrey; and the chawbacons who carry the produce of their acres to it, instead of to the neighbouring village of London, retain much of their pristine barbarity. The town furnishes an interesting scene on a hunting morning, particularly on a Saturday. At an early hour, groups of grinning cits may be seen pouring in from the London side, some on the top of Cloud's coaches, some in taxed carts, but the greater number mounted on good serviceable-looking nags, of the invaluable species, calculated for sport or business, 'warranted free from vice, and quiet both to ride and in harness …', and thus they onward jog, until the sign of the Greyhound, stretching quite across the main street, greets their expectant optics.' Later, 'they arrived at the end of the first stage on the road to the hunt, namely the small town of Croydon, the rendezvous of London sportsmen. The whole place was alive with red coats, green coats, blue coats, black coats, brown coats, in short, coats of all the colours of the rainbow.'

Hunting continued in the area until the spread of urban development early in the 20th century. The last meets in Croydon would have been at Shirley or Addington but they have continued in nearby rural areas such as Chelsham into recent years.

The lonely highways could be quite dangerous places even as late as the early 19th century. Smuggling still occurred and there are local records of highwaymen stopping, robbing and even killing people on the roads in 1811 and 1813. In 1836 a gang of highwaymen was reported to be operating in the area, stopping farmers and treating them brutally on their way home from Croydon market.

At the beginning of the 19th century the inhabitants of Norwood were mostly farmers and labourers, with a large population of gypsies who pitched their tents in the oak woods and on the furze-clad wastes. After the enclosures, building development began to spread over the area and the gypsies gradually moved elsewhere. They were well established on the Norwood heights at least by the 17th century, as an entry in Pepys' diary dated 11 August 1668 shows, ' This afternoon my wife and Mercer and Deb went with Pelling to see the gypsies at Lambeth and had their fortunes told.' Much of Norwood was, of course, in the parish of Lambeth.

In his *Reminiscences of a Country Journalist* published in 1886, Thomas Frost states that the gypsies

> were in the habit of camping every summer in large numbers upon the patches of waste bordering the lanes that intersected the woods of Anerley and Penge. The men made clothes-pegs and butchers' wooden skewers, which were hawked through the neighbouring villages and hamlets by brown-faced boys and girls, or perambulated the vicinity with the treadle-wheel and fire-basket of the itinerant tinker and knife-grinder. Some who had acquired or inherited a little money, made the round of the country fairs as horse-dealers, not without incurring the suspicion that they sometimes sold horses which they had not bought or bred. The women practised palmistry, in which their reputation was so great as to furnish Monmouth Street publishers with the title, *The Norwood Gipsy Fortune-Teller*, a little book in great demand among young women of all classes.

Gypsies still appear in the area from time to time but their homes are likely to be in caravans and they no longer camp in the Great North Wood!

Milling

Standing at the headwaters of the River Wandle, mills were for centuries part of the local scene. The River Wandle has two main sources, at Croydon and at Carshalton, and falls, on average, about fourteen feet per mile in its nine-mile long course to the Thames at Wandsworth. The river was of no use for navigation but was very efficient at providing water-power for mills. It was important to the local economy as at various times there were mills for

37 *By 1924 Waddon Mill was one of only four still working on the River Wandle. In 1928 it was grinding 100 tons of wheat daily but it ceased work in that year. The mill pond seen here was filled in during the 1960s and is now a car park.*

38 *Allen's flour mill in St James's Road near Spurgeon's Bridge was similar to many steam-powered mills that gradually replaced the windmills as demand for flour increased.*

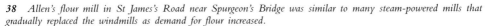

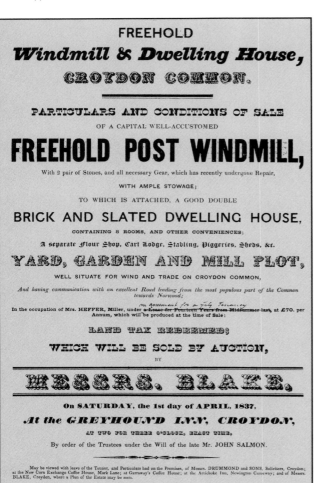

FREEHOLD
Windmill & Dwelling House,
CROYDON COMMON.

———

PARTICULARS AND CONDITIONS OF SALE

OF A CAPITAL WELL-ACCUSTOMED

FREEHOLD POST WINDMILL,

With 2 pair of Stones, and all necessary Gear, which has recently undergone Repair,

WITH AMPLE STOWAGE;

TO WHICH IS ATTACHED, A GOOD DOUBLE

BRICK AND SLATED DWELLING HOUSE,

CONTAINING 8 ROOMS, AND OTHER CONVENIENCES;

A separate Flour Shop, Cart Lodge, Stabling, Piggeries, Sheds, &c.

YARD, GARDEN AND MILL PLOT,

WELL SITUATE FOR WIND AND TRADE ON CROYDON COMMON,

*And having communication with an excellent Road leading from the most populous part of the Common
towards Norwood;*

In the occupation of Mrs. HEFFER, Miller, under a Lease for Fourteen Years from Midsummer last, at £70. per
Annum, which will be produced at the time of Sale;

LAND TAX REDEEMED;

WHICH WILL BE SOLD BY AUCTION,

BY

MESSRS. BLAKE,

On SATURDAY, the 1st day of APRIL, 1837,

At the GREYHOUND INN, CROYDON,

AT TWO FOR THREE O'CLOCK, EXACT TIME,

By order of the Trustees under the Will of the late Mr. JOHN SALMON.

May be viewed with leave of the Tenant, and Particulars had on the Premises, of Messrs. DRUMMOND and SONS, Solicitors, Croydon;
at the New Corn Exchange Coffee House, Mark Lane; at Garraway's Coffee House; at the Artichoke Inn, Newington Causeway; and of Messrs.
BLAKE, Croydon, where a Plan of the Estate may be seen.

39 *Sale particulars from 1837 for the 'Black Windmill' which was bought by John Richardson, uncle to John Ruskin.*

corn, working copper, iron, oil, leather, paper, snuff, gunpowder, and for printing textiles. Domesday Book records a mill at Croydon and there were several in the parish by the early 19th century. The water-mill at Waddon continued to grind corn until as late as 1928.

Windmills are recorded from the 12th century onwards, and it is believed one stood near the top of Crown Hill, but documentary evidence is not available. Near Broad Green stood Croydon Windmill, on the north side of the appropriately named Windmill Road, at the junction with St James's Road. It is shown on John Rocque's map and on the Enclosure map, and was held by William Gardiner from about 1790. Entries in the Croydon rate books for William Gardiner's mill cease in 1814 but continue for John Salmon's, later referred to as the 'Black Mill', and it may be that the fairly common practice of demolishing a mill and re-using parts happened here. The 'Black Mill' stood in the angle of Gloucester and Sydenham Roads, fifty yards back from the latter and about one hundred and thirty yards from the road junction. It was a post-mill with a roundhouse, and in 1837 it was purchased by George Richardson, baker, an uncle of John Ruskin. By 1855 a Croydon directory records it as 'to let' and it must have been demolished soon afterwards as it does not appear on the 1862 Ordnance Survey map.

About 1829 a smock mill at Halstead in Kent was taken down and parts were used in a new mill erected on Croydon Common. This stood about one hundred and twenty yards north of Windmill Road, on the site of Beulah Grove. The mill was six storeys high, and stood on a square brick base. It was a typical Kentish smock-mill with eight sides, and the weatherboarding was presumably painted with white lead, as it became known as the 'White Mill'. The mill was sold in 1860 and demolished soon afterwards.

The last mill to be erected on Croydon Common (and one of the last in Surrey) was Noake's Mill, first recorded in the rate book for 1852. This was a tower windmill of six floors and stood approximately in the centre of the triangle formed by Gloucester Road, the railway and the section of Neville Road turning west off Gloucester Road. It had a very short life of ten to fifteen years, being offered for sale in 1858, and a few years later was recorded as disused.

Another windmill recorded in Croydon rate book for 1812 was prominently situated at Upper Norwood on Westow Hill, about fifty yards south of the *Woodman* public house in Woodman Road. It is not known whether it was a tower or post-mill, and it ceased work in 1853, being demolished soon afterwards.

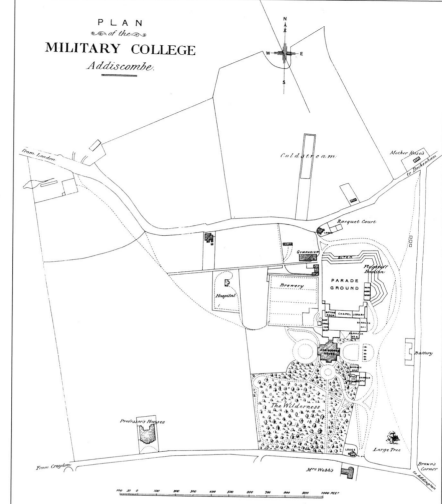

40 Addiscombe Place was built to replace an earlier house about 1701. It was acquired by the Honourable East India Company and opened as a military training college for its army in 1809. This plan shows the layout of the grounds. In 1861, following the Indian Mutiny, the company's military organisation was disbanded. Woolwich and Sandhurst were considered adequate for officer training purposes. Addiscombe College closed in August of that year and the estate was sold to the British Land Company. The mansion and most of the buildings were demolished and the five roads named Canning, Clyde, Elgin, Havelock and Outram were laid out on the site. Although all had Indian connections, none of those named was educated here.

41 Some of the barrack blocks at Addiscombe, c.1859.

Coulsdon Common at one time had two wind-mills. The earlier and smaller mill was shown on Rocque's map and stood on the north side of Stites Hill Road, where Windmill House now stands. The second dated from a few years later and was about a hundred yards away on the south side of Stites Hill Road in an enclosure on the common opposite Windmill Cottage. Both were post-mills and the smaller ceased to work in the mid-19th century and was demolished in the 1880s: the other ceased working in 1893 and was demolished in the 1920s.

A mill was recorded at Addington in 1292 and one was last shown on maps in the early 18th century. It stood approximately one thousand yards south of the church on the west side of Lodge Lane opposite the present fire station.

The last windmill in Croydon, fortunately still surviving, is at Shirley, just off Upper Shirley Road

42 'Mother' Rose with Addiscombe cadets at her cottage in August 1859. She was born Dorcas Letts, the daughter of a farm labourer, at Coulsdon in 1809. She married John Rose, a farm labourer, when she was 27 and they moved into the cottage in 1840. The cottage, typical of many farm workers' houses in Croydon at the time, stood in Lower Addiscombe Road where it is now joined by Inglis Road. It had only two rooms, and the cadets used to visit and smoke (not permitted at the college), and sing the latest songs. She sold them such things as bread and butter, milk and eggs, but no strong drink. She kept order and discipline with a small cane, which she had no hesitation in using if the language became too strong. She was greatly respected by the cadets.

in a small new housing development, Postmill Close. Dating from about 1855, it is a tower mill, but replaced a post-mill built around 1809 and destroyed by fire in 1854. The Alwen family were the millers here until 1884 and the mill continued working into the 1890s. It lay derelict for many years but was renovated and cared for by local inhabitants until Croydon Corporation bought it in 1952 and incorporated it in the grounds of the new John Ruskin school, since demolished. It is now cared for by trustees. Much of the machinery is intact and there are frequent open days.

43   This drawing of the Black Horse *at Addiscombe in about 1820 is by James Bourne. The hostelry was much frequented by the Addiscombe cadets. Col. Vibart related the following story about an incident here: 'There was an ex-prize fighter named "Pretty Agent". This man had a very unpleasant habit of going into the pubs, taking the glasses of other people, lowering the contents down his own throat, and, if remonstrated with, a knock-down blow was the immediate result. Well this fellow on this particular occasion met his match. It was after the dismissal from parade one afternoon that many of the cadets made for the toll-gate at Woodside, where there was to be a little 'sprinting' with some of the running men of Croydon. This sport necessarily brought a fair sample of the roughs of the place, and amongst them 'Pretty Agent'. The* Black Horse *was the rendezvous and of course several of the cadets found their way in, and were quickly and quietly served by old John Grey, the landlord. No sooner were the glasses put on the counter than "Pretty Agent" took up one, but was prevented drinking the contents by one of the cadets called Paddy F— who seized him, and challenged him to come outside and fight. This he readily accepted, no doubt thinking he would easily floor his man; but he was doomed to bitter disappointment, for Paddy F— soon "shaped", and landed a drive from the right on the nose, following it up with a swinger from the left which sent him rolling into the ditch. This passage of arms effectually prevented the ruffian from ever again molesting the cadets.'*

No illustrations are known of the early Croydon windmills, which must have formed an impressive sight on Croydon Common in the mid-19th century. They were no doubt brought into use to serve the growing population but steam mills were already being built. More followed in the second half of the century. One of the largest was Allen's in St James's Road. Its tall silo was a familiar landmark from the 1920s until the 1950s, when it was replaced by the large Wonderloaf Bakery, which was in turn replaced by housing in the 1980s.

The Woe Water

Intermittent streams and springs are quite common in chalk downland areas. Usually known as bournes, they are caused by rain collecting in the chalk which acts as a sort of sponge. After excessive rainfall the level rises and overflows cause a bourne to appear in a normally dry area.

The North Downs south of Croydon include what is one of the most dramatic series of dry valleys in the country, no doubt originally containing streams which fed the River Wandle.

44   *Croydon Theatre in Crown Hill was built in about 1800. Garrow describes it as 'neatly fitted up with upper and lower boxes, pit and gallery, nearly on the plans of the London Houses. Not many towns, perhaps, in the country, have a theatre exceeding this in neatness and convenience.' By 1838 it had become the home of the Croydon Literary and Scientific Institution and a new theatre was erected on the site in the 1860s.*

Both the Caterham and the Smitham Bottom valleys were flooded every few years by the rising of the Bourne or 'woe-water' as it was often called. It gained a reputation far afield for portending national disasters and the effect of the flood waters in Croydon's low-lying Old Town area was usually disastrous, bringing disease and woe.

The first record of a bourne in the locality is in 1473, when John Warkworth, Master of Peter-house, Cambridge gave it the character of ill omen by describing it as a Woe-water. In Camden's *Britannia* of 1586 the following appears: 'For the torrent that the vulgar affirm to rise here sometimes and to presage dearth and pestilence; it seems hardly worth so much as the mentioning tho' perhaps it may have some truth in it.'

Daniel Defoe in *A Tour thro' the whole Island of Great Britain divided into Circuits or Journies*, 1724-6, writes, 'This put me in mind that the very same thing is said to happen at Smitham Bottom in Surrey, beyond Croydon, and that the Water gushing out of the chalky Hills about eight miles from Croydon on the road to Ryegate, fills the whole Bottom, and makes a large River just to the Town's End of Croydon; and then turning to the Left runs into the River which rises in the Town, and runs

to Carshalton; and I name it, because the Country People here have exactly the same Notion, that this water never breaks out but against a Famine; and as I am sure it has not now broken out for more than fifty Years, it may, for ought I know, be true.'

John Corbet Anderson gives the following detailed description in *A Short Chronicle Concerning the Parish of Croydon*, published in 1882:

The springs of those tributary heads of the Wandle which arose from under the western side of High Street, and fed the Scarbrook, were powerful. A noted spring of water also formerly gushed up opposite the west end of

45   *William Page has left a description of Croydon Fair, which is depicted here in 1833: 'This being kept as a high festival great preparations were made by nearly all folks in brightening up the outside and insides of their houses in order, to receive all friends and relations … The town was a fair of itself, music, singing, acrobats, and all kinds of entertainments going on in the streets, and an immense traffic of all kinds of vehicles passing and repassing through the place … That well-known hostelry, the Greyhound, conducted by the gentlemanly and lamented Mr Thos. Boon, where upwards of 100 geese and a goodly number of pigs and ducks being provided and consumed … the second day exhibited a different aspect from the first, being attended by many of the gentry of Croydon and its neighbourhood bringing their families, whose carriages reached from Coombe Street in Park Lane to George Street, making expensive purchases of elegant articles which were not to be had at the shops of Croydon or elsewhere, except in London or Paris; these expensive things being sold at pretty stalls or small bazaars kept by French women, and most picturesque they looked in their high handkerchief turbans, with long red gold ear rings reaching and touching their shoulders …'*

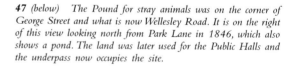

46 (above) Beulah Spa was opened in 1831 but had only a short life, the counter-attractions of the nearby Crystal Palace leading to its closure in 1858. Designed by the famous architect, Decimus Burton, the features included a camera obscura, a maze, a circus ring, two lakes, the spa-well and a refreshment room. Events included dancing, archery, fortune-telling, firework displays, concerts and ballooning. Much of the site remains as the Lawns open space.

47 (below) The Pound for stray animals was on the corner of George Street and what is now Wellesley Road. It is on the right of this view looking north from Park Lane in 1846, which also shows a pond. The land was later used for the Public Halls and the underpass now occupies the site.

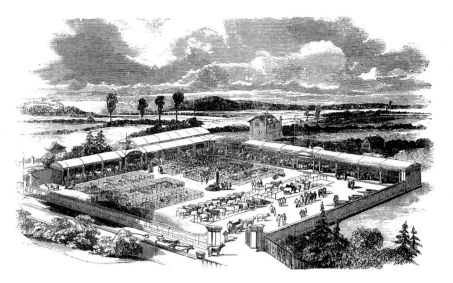

48 *This new Cattle Market was opened at Selsdon Road in 1850. It had accommodation for 1,400 sheep and pigs, with sheds for 200 calves and stands for 200 head of cattle. The* Illustrated London News *reported that 'It will doubtless continue to be well attended by the respectable butchers of London, and must prove beneficial to the farmers and graziers of Surrey, Sussex and Kent, being of easy access from the railways traversing those counties.' It closed in 1935.*

Sheldon Street, and a reminiscence of it still lingers in the name Pump-Pail. Benson Spring likewise was a fine and very clear one: this arose about fifty feet north of the water-works' engine house, and the path leading to it from Surrey Street used to be called Spring Walk: another path that led from Surrey Street to this spring is represented by Sturt's Yard. Benson Spring was never frozen over, not even in the year when the Thames was frozen: it is the source of the present water works.

With respect to that other tributary of the Wandle which flowed from the southern end of the parish, this stream ran along the Brighton Road, between the footpath on the west, and the roadway. Arrived at the Anchor it coursed along the passage at the back of that inn, running immediately alongside the wall on the east, yet leaving a space of ground four or five feet wide, in front of the doors of those little ancient tenements which still face the passage. The stream continued its course for a short distance along what is now the path on the west side of Southbridge Lane, when crossing the road, and entering the meadow, it separated into two branches, one of which ran through the field, while the other skirted the east side of Southbridge Lane. As it gurgled through the meadow, the bourne appeared a lovely rivulet, about five feet wide, and from one to two feet deep, with a nice gravelly bottom for trout to spawn in; and here, sixty years ago, they used to catch trout a foot long. The eastern fork of

the stream flowing round by the line of St Andrew's Street [which, however, at that time had no existence] eventually met the western branch of the stream in front of, where now is, the north door of St. Andrew's Church; and at this point, a wide plank, with a single hand-rail on a couple of posts, was thrown across the stream, to enable our Croydonians to pass dry-shod in the direction of Coombe Lane.

A little further on, just opposite the N.W. angle of St. Andrew's School, the stream was spanned by another bridge, called the 'Six Arches Bridge'; for here, over the water one had to cross to get to Meadow Stile. At this point the bourne was some twenty feet in breadth, and the bridge, constructed of brick, about three feet wide, with handrails, was placed obliquely to the stream. Doubtless it is to one or other of these now defunct bridges that we are indebted for a nomenclature still preserved in South-bridge Lane, South-bridge Place, etc. A third bridge, also regularly built of brick, with a parapet of the same material, communicated between Pump-pail and Duppa's Hill Lane, for it was a main route.

And now the stream ran close under the west wall of the old Running Horse, one of the windows of which, supported on posts, projected over the minnowy flood; nor could the front entrance of this hostelry be gained, except by a wooden bridge; another tiny bridge led to the skittle ground. Having parted again, in order to encircle 'Bog Island,' eventually the

49 *The Royal Masonic Benevolent Institution for Aged Freemasons and their Widows provided this fine Asylum alongside the railway just north of Windmill Bridge. Unusually the frontage faced the railway lines. It was consecrated at a ceremony in Croydon Town Hall on 1 August 1850. The party went on to St James's Church to hear a sermon and then joined a procession of a band, boys and girls from Masonic Institutions, and several hundred freemasons, which proceeded to the asylum. The building is now used as an old people's home.*

combined stream arrived at the old churchyard, when deviating towards the west, its waters mingled with those from the Scarbrook and formed the Wandle.

On the rising of the bourne, which on average happened every fourth or fifth year, the Old Town used to be inundated, so much so, that the natives had to cross over the road on planks, to get from the houses on one side of the road to those on the other; and this condition of affairs lasted sometimes five or six weeks. Meanwhile the water on the Brighton Road, in the neighbourhood of Purley Oaks, reached even up to the horses' girths. At Pump pail burial ground, in those palmy sanitary times that preceded extra-mural sepulture, coffins have been seen to float, and actually required to be forced under water while they were shovelling the earth into the grave! Fancy the inhabitants of neighbouring houses or ourselves being compelled to drink water that had been filtered through such a process! Cremation itself would be preferable. In Boswell Court House, old Kilmister saw a servant at the cellardoor get into a floating tub, and push herself with a stick across to where the barrel stood, in order to draw the beer; 'this,' said he, 'happened when the bourne was up, yet the adjoining roadway was dry'.

The Caterham Bourne rises near Wapses Lodge roundabout, and the Coulsdon Bourne near the *Red Lion* at Coulsdon. Bourne flows have continued

to cause problems over the years. That of 1904 was particularly notable. In March there was extensive flooding along Godstone Road and a five-year-old schoolboy, Tommy Wells of Wyche Grove, was drowned in a flooded gravel pit near the *Windsor Castle* in Brighton Road. The *Coulsdon & Purley Weekly Record* reported on 16 January 1904 that

> The Bourne water this week caused serious damage. On Friday the water rose to an abnormal height, filling the large basin reserved for excess water of the Surrey Water Company, and, rushing across the road, flooded Mr Bridgeland's yard, and also that of the District Council, the water coming up to the axles of the wheels of the various carts standing in the yard. On Sunday quite exciting scenes were witnessed, as the water, coming across the road flooded many gardens … The Bourne has made its appearance as far along the road to Croydon as the tramway shed. It is appearing in volume on the Smitham side of the Surrey Water Company's premises, flooding the cellars of many of the houses. We fear the development of this popular district will be temporarily retarded through these singular floods … Hundreds of visitors have come to Purley to witness this extraordinary watery phenomenon.

Spasmodic bourne flows continued throughout the 20th century but the most spectacular since 1904 was during the very wet autumn and winter of 2000-1. The A22 Godstone Road at Whyteleafe was flooded to the depth of two feet on 12 December 2000 and this important main road had to be closed for some weeks. Numerous premises were flooded and people were seen in boats, with children paddling in the water. Cellars in South Croydon near the *Swan and Sugar Loaf* were flooded. The 'woe water' can still bring its share of trouble.

Water Supply and Drainage Problems

The springs and ponds of the Old Town area provided the water needed by the townspeople until the mid-19th century. There was no proper drainage and the periodic rising of the bourne and frequent flooding resulted in sewage and general rubbish being present in the water used for drinking. Several quotations give us a hint of conditions in the town before the Victorian period. King Henry VIII is reputed to have said, when speaking of somewhere he disliked, 'This house standeth low, and is rheumatick, like unto Croydon, where I never could be without sickness.' In Elizabethan times a notice stated that, 'The streets were deep hollow ways and very dirty, the houses generally with wooden steps into them, and darkened by large trees growing before them – and the inhabitants in general were smiths and colliers.' The houses were no doubt raised to avoid the periodic flooding.

There is little doubt that the town would have prospered more had there not been major problems wih lack of sanitation and pollution, which increased as the population grew. By the 1840s conditions in the town were deplorable, but similar unhygienic conditions prevailed throughout the country. Croydon probably lagged little behind other towns and cities but no attempt had as yet been made to provide a proper drainage system or a communal piped water supply. Outbreaks of cholera, typhoid and other diseases were commonplace.

A national sanitary campaign had started in 1839 and a Royal Commission on the Health of Towns published reports in 1844 and 1845. Some local people were anxious to see sanitary improve-

ments but it was not until the passing of the Public Health Act in 1848 that much progress was made. The Act aimed at 'improving the sanitary conditions of towns and populous places in England and Wales' and provided for the setting up of a General Board of Health with responsibility for Local Boards who were as far as practicable to have comprehensive control and management of such matters as water supply, sewerage, drainage, cleansing, paving and burial. The inhabitants of Croydon soon submitted the necessary petition and a preliminary public enquiry was held at the Town Hall in March 1849, conducted by Mr William Ranger C.E. In his subsequent report Dr Westall, later Honorary Medical Officer to the Local Board of Health, stated:

> In the lower parts dense fogs prevail and hang upon the surface in the vicinity of Southbridge and Bog Island, whilst at and near Waddon there are marshes, with stagnant ditches from 12 to 15 feet wide, charged with animal and vegetable matter, from which noxious exhalations are conveyed by the prevailing winds to the town; moreover the town itself is entirely devoid of under-drainage and therefore dependent on a surface drainage, which is a source of unhealthy exhalations, giving rise to epidemics which have of late years greatly increased.

Mr G. Penfold, Clerk to the Improvement Commissioners, stated:

> The inhabitants throw their sullage into the public drains in the street, not intended for that purpose; consequently the streets are constantly in a filthy state, and the drains still more so.'
>
> Those enormous reservoirs for the reception of filth, called Laud's and Scarbrook Ponds, have been used from time immemorial to receive the sullage of the town as well as that from slaughter-houses and private dwellings. Laud's Pond is not only an abominable nuisance at all times, but must be the means of creating fevers

50 (facing page) This plan of the streams and ponds of Old Town shows their position in relation to the present road layout. Those marked with an x had gone by 1838, and the remainder, except for the River Wandle north of the railway, had gone by 1850.

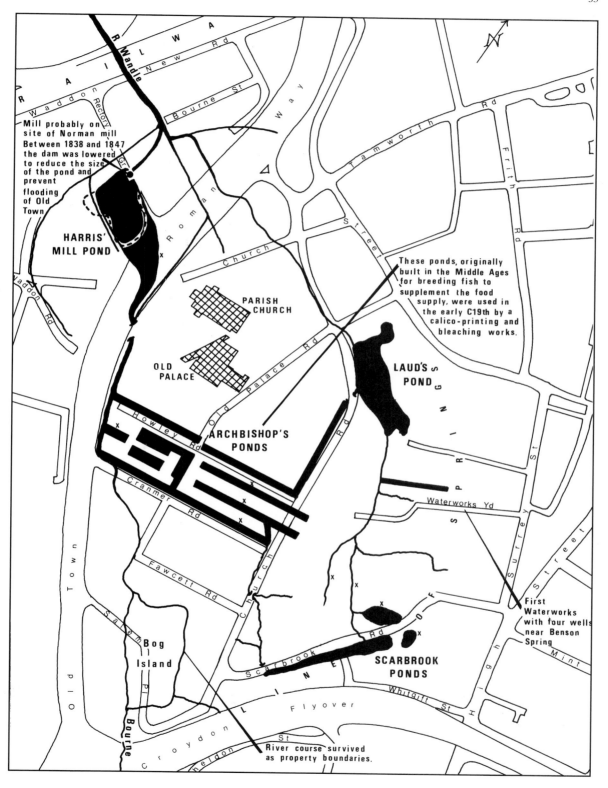

Mill probably on site of Norman mill Between 1838 and 1847 the dam was lowered to reduce the size of the pond and prevent flooding of Old Town

HARRIS' MILL POND

These ponds, originally built in the Middle Ages for breeding fish to supplement the food supply, were used in the early C19th by a calico-printing and bleaching works.

PARISH CHURCH

OLD PALACE

LAUD'S POND

ARCHBISHOP'S PONDS

Waterworks Yd

First Waterworks with four wells near Benson Spring

Bog Island

SCARBROOK PONDS

River course survived as property boundaries.

51   This view shows Laud's Pond from Church Road in 1849. A number of industrial buildings, granaries, etc. can be seen between the pond and the higher ground beyond, where the second Town Hall is a conspicuous landmark. The pond was drained in 1850 as part of the scheme for providing proper drainage and a good water supply.

and other diseases. The stench from it is very bad, and in the Summer unbearable.

Scarbrook Pond is an able seconder to Laud's Pond in their joint occupation of spreading fever and death among the inhabitants .

Ranger's report also contained the following:

I think there are not more than 300 water-closets in the whole parish, the residue consisting of common privies; many of which are placed in situations regardless of ordinary decency and convenience, producing the most serious consequences to the inhabitants.

The average of privies among the poorer classes is not above one to three houses, many of these houses containing several families.

In several yards and courts at the south end of High Street and in the district of South-bridge, Pump-pail, Union Street, Mill Street and the Old Town generally … the privies are all open, overhanging the watercourse and … a child visiting such a place some time since, fell through and was drowned.

In some of the better houses in High Street:

The privies are situated in the lower apartments, some in cellars, others leading into the kitchens with no means of getting rid of the soil except by bringing it through the house. In other houses the soil of their neighbours' privies is continually oozing, and permeating the walls of adjoining houses, producing the most noxious and offensive smells.

The district of Surrey Street with its yards, the Middle Row, Huson's Court, Market Street, Bell Hill and yards and Scarbrook Hill, if brought before you in all their disgusting wretchedness of filth, open dunghills and cesspools, dilapidated privies, with water deficient in quantity and bad in quality, would be but a twice-told tale, and their reiteration irksome.

Dr Westall showed that out of 1,550 houses in the parish, water supplies were as follows:

775 are not supplied at all; 275 complain that water is not good and the supply insufficient. The occupants of 14 houses are obliged to buy beer to get water from the landlord's pump; and in the Old Town, out of 213 houses, 143 are deficient in supply, and 24 find the water unfit for use.

52 Scarbrook Pond was another of the ponds and watercourses drained and filled in by the Local Board of Health in 1850. This print shows nearby hovels.

53 The new waterworks reservoir at Park Hill was opened at a ceremony on 11 December 1851. This print shows the large crowd which descended into the reservoir by means of a temporary staircase. The Archbishop of Canterbury led a prayer that the waters would prove a spiritual as well as a temporal blessing. The reservoir was a circular domed structure 75 feet in diameter, capable of holding 950,000 gallons of water. It was disused after 1923 and was filled with rubble on safety grounds in the 1960s.

54   Cuthbert William Johnson was born at Lee in 1799 and moved to Croydon in 1848. He was a barrister and already familiar with Croydon's problems. He was a colleague of Edwin Chadwick, the sanitary reformer, and like him was a member of the Metropolitan Commission of Sewers. Cuthbert Johnson, an agricultural journalist, was appointed first chairman of the Local Board of Health. His great interest in sewage irrigation eventually led to the establishment of Croydon's sewage farms at Beddington and South Norwood. He died in 1878 and was buried in St Peter's churchyard.

The Inspector's report concluded:

> It has been shown in the evidence that the whole of the inhabitants have no other means of obtaining supplies of water except by pumping or fetching from a distant source … The cost, in some instances, for fetching water amounts to 2/6d … per week per house.'
>
> The district comprised in the Croydon Union is at present the most unhealthy in the county … the proportion of deaths to the population in the more healthy districts was 1 in 58, whilst in the Croydon district it was as high as 1 in 36.

It recommended the application of the Public Health Act to Croydon, which was one of the first 15 towns in the country where the powers were conferred by Provisional Order on 1 August 1849. The others were Carmarthen, Chatham, Coventry, Durham, Gloucester, Kendal, Lancaster, Leicester, New Windsor, Sheerness, Taunton, Uxbridge, Ware and Worcester.

The new Croydon Local Board of Health was elected and commenced work in September 1849. Within two years it had planned and constructed a waterworks pumping station in Surrey Street, a large underground reservoir at Park Hill, a sewage works and miles of water mains and sewers. The ponds and streams were filled in, a culvert constructed to take the bourne underground, the mill-dam near the church was removed and all the open privies and cesspools abolished. Some 1,300 water closets were provided, water and sewer connections made to 1,700 houses, footways improved and road drainage provided. These benefits were confined to a Special District forming the central part of the parish. The Lambeth Water Company was already in process of providing a water supply to parts of Norwood within the parish.

The new waterworks were ceremoniously opened by the Archbishop of Canterbury on 11 December 1851. Unfortunately a typhoid outbreak hit the town in 1852. There were 2,000 cases and 57 deaths. This was undoubtedly due to early problems with the new works. The town became a battleground for civic litigation and for engineering matters such as tubular stoneware drains, sewage disposal methods, and sewer ventilation. The Local Board's speedy actions and works did much to advance the cause of sanitary science, however, and the foundations were well and truly laid for the future expansion and development of Croydon into one of the most healthy towns in the country. When the town became a borough in 1883 the legend appropriately adopted for the coat of arms was 'Sanitate Crescamus' – 'Let us grow in health'.

VI

Victorian Progress 1851-1901

THE YEAR 1851 saw the Great Exhibition of Science and Industry take place in the Crystal Palace in Hyde Park. As an exhibition it was undoubtedly a great success but it failed to succeed in its aims of fostering trade and international relations. No doubt many Croydonians visited the exhibition and were captivated by the great glass edifice which has somehow come to symbolise the Victorian age. Only three years later the building was re-erected in a much enlarged form on the Norwood heights, just across the road from the Croydon boundary. Its presence attracted much building development in the adjacent areas. Large detached villas in spacious grounds soon spread through Upper Norwood as wealthy Londoners made their homes near the Palace.

The town of Croydon now had a Local Board of Health, a good water supply, and a drainage and sewage disposal system which was held up as a model for other towns to follow. It was poised to develop at a faster rate than almost any other town in the land, the population growing from 20,343 in 1851, to 30,240 in 1861, and to 134,037 by 1901. But it was still a largely self-contained town, surrounded by open country, and remained so until beyond the end of the century.

Gray's Commercial & General Directory of Croydon for 1853, which would probably have been compiled the previous year, states, 'There is a cattle market on Thursdays; great improvements have been made for the accommodation of persons frequenting it, by the erection of a new enclosed market, with all convenient appurtenances, near the site of the old cattle pens, between the Brighton and Selsdon roads. The Corn Market on Saturdays, is held in the lower

55 In the early 1850s great activity was taking place in the hamlet of Penge just beyond the Croydon borders. Large numbers of navvies were rebuilding the Crystal Palace on a scale much enlarged from the building in Hyde Park. It was opened by Queen Victoria on 10 June 1854. This view shows it in the early days before the north transept on the right was destroyed by fire in 1866. Generations of Croydonians enjoyed the Crystal Palace until its destruction by fire in 1936.

56   The Queen's Hotel (left) in Church Road, Upper Norwood was built for the convenience of visitors to the Crystal Palace. Upper Norwood became a very fashionable suburb and was at the height of its popularity when this photograph was taken around 1900.

court of the Town Hall. The market for Butter, Poultry, Fruit, etc. being held on the same day, in the Market-house, opposite the *Greyhound* hotel. The Fairs are on the 5th of July and the 2nd of October, the latter being very numerously attended, both for business in horses, sheep, and cattle, and by pleasure seekers. A Fair for Wool is usually held early in July, and the Sheep and Lamb Fair in August. Croydon is the place of Election for Members of Parliament for the Eastern Division of the County; and the Summer Assizes are held alternately with Guildford, when, besides the criminal cases, a very heavy 'cause list' usually keeps the town in a state of considerably increased bustle for a fortnight or three weeks.' The directory lists new parish churches at St Peter's (Croham, 1851), Christ Church (Broad Green, 1852), St Mark's (Norwood-by-Railway, now South Norwood, 1852) and Shirley Chapel-of-Ease. There were several nonconformist chapels. Also listed are a number of Religious and Benevolent Societies, including Croydon Coal Charity

(established 1838), Croydon Clothing Society (established 1830), Croydon Dispensary (established 1835) and the Croydon Savings Bank (established 1819). The Victorian zeal for good works was already evident and as the town grew so did the number of charitable organisations.

Education was becoming more widespread during this period. Croydon British School had been established in 1812 and a Ragged School was opened in 1846. There was at least one Dame School serving the village of Shirley and there were several church schools and about a dozen private schools, some taking boarders. The Friends School had moved to Park Lane from Islington in 1825. Despite the efforts of the Local Board of Health there were several outbreaks of typhoid and other fevers in the 1850s, '60s and '70s. These led the Society of Friends

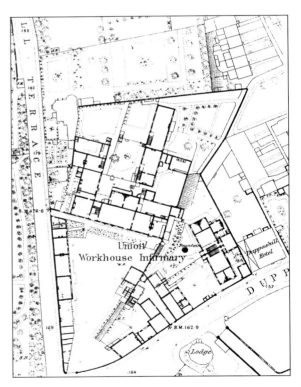

57   Croydon Workhouse was built at Duppas Hill in 1727. It was a large structure but no illustration is known. This plan shows the location and area of the buildings as existing in 1868. By this time it was being used only as the union infirmary, a new workhouse having been built at Queen's Road and opened in 1866.

58 *This photograph of a ward in the union infirmary at Duppas Hill dates from about 1865. The notice on the wall reads: 'Visitors are prohibited from giving any type of work to the patients without the special permission of the matron'. The building was demolished after the new Union Infirmary was opened at Mayday Road in 1885.*

59 *Croydon's new workhouse was almost complete when this photograph was taken in 1865. As many as 2,800 inmates were housed here in winter, and about 1,500 in summer. The able-bodied paupers were put to work stone-breaking, while the women and children did cleaning, laundry and sewing. The tower and central part of the building remains but the wings no longer exist.*

60 *The 1868 edition of the six inch to the mile Ordnance Survey map shows a marked contrast with the Enclosure Maps on pages 30 and 33. The town had already spread out over many of the surrounding fields and woods but the countryside still reached well into it. The railways had cut swathes through the open land. The population reached 55,652 in 1871 and was growing fast.*

61 *Croydon General Hospital was established by public subscription in 1867. The 14 beds of this newly founded paying hospital were housed in the union infirmary from 1867 to 1873, the cost of a bed being five shillings a week, although a few were free. It then moved and opened with 30 beds at Oakfield Lodge in London Road, formerly a private house in extensive grounds. This photograph dates from the 1880s and shows Oakfield Lodge before later extensions. The hospital closed in 1996.*

to move their school from Croydon to Saffron Walden in 1879 but had little impact on general urban development, which proceeded apace.

Forster's Education Act of 1870 led to the setting up of the Croydon School Board in 1871. The Board took over several existing schools and opened new ones at Bynes Road (Purley Oaks), and Oval Road two years later. These schools were non-sectarian, though there was much jostling between Anglicans and nonconformists for places on the Board. Fees were charged even though attendance was compulsory.

School log books record many fascinating details of life and conditions at the time. In 1876 Brighton Road Girls School recorded that 'Kelly and Collins were playing about shoeless, nearly naked'. The same school recorded absentees watching ploughing matches and gleaning! The summer break was called Harvest Holiday, even in the town schools such as Parish Church and Oval. At Addington National School, still in the heart of the country, children walked long distances from Coombe, Sanderstead, Selsdon, Fairchildes, Fickles Hole, Ham Farm, Spring Park and Shirley. When heavy snow started to fall in school hours the vicar called to send children straight home. The youngest left school in the

autumn and did not return until spring. Some of the older boys left school for the summer months to work for the farmers, as cowherds, etc., returning in October for the winter. May Day was still celebrated widely and this is confirmed by log book entries such as 'the usual absences of several boys carrying away garlands', 'many absent garlanding', and 'a small attendance because of maypolling'.

In his unpublished thesis, *Some Aspects of the Urban Development of Croydon*, Dr R.C.W. Cox explains that 19th-century development in the town was largely self-contained. Building plots were purchased mainly by Croydon men, who employed Croydon builders to develop the land. Because so much of the development was on a small scale, social segregation of housing was not very apparent. The Waldrons, originally part of the Haling Park estate, was bought by Edward Vigers, who in 1850 sold individual building plots to gentlemen who employed their own architects. It was laid out as a private estate with two ornate lodges, where green-liveried gatekeepers in top hats opened the gate when requested, but admitted no undesirable persons. One lodge and some of the houses remain in the conservation area. Only a few yards away down the hill were the slums of Old Town. Almost

62   In 1881 the Board of Guardians decided to build a new union infirmary in Mayday Road, not far from the union house. The opening took place on 16 May 1885 in the presence of the Archbishop of Canterbury, Dr Benson. This postcard view dates from about 1910. It is now Mayday University Hospital and has been greatly extended in recent years.

63   Dr Alfred Carpenter was born in 1825. He became well known both locally and nationally as a pioneer in sanitary science. He was a member of the Local Board of Health from 1859 until his election as President of the British Medical Association in 1879. Later he was a member of the borough council. An energetic advocate of preventative medicine, he was influential in the establishment of public baths in the town, the siting of the gas works at Waddon away from the town centre, and in the establishment of public slaughterhouses. He was at various times president of the Croydon School of Art, the Croydon Temperance Society and the Croydon Microscopical and Natural History Club, chairman of the Whitgift Foundation, a JP, and medical adviser to four successive archbishops of Canterbury. He died in 1892.

invariably the better class of housing was to be found on the higher ground, but the general spread of lower-middle-class properties often included patches of working-class housing. New parishes were created as housing spread.

Opportunities for local employment also increased as small factories and workshops were built to cater for the growing population. Brewing was already well established and, on a larger scale, carriage building was an important activity. A

THE PORTUGAL.

THE SARDINIAN.

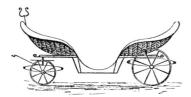

THE QUEEN'S PATTERN.

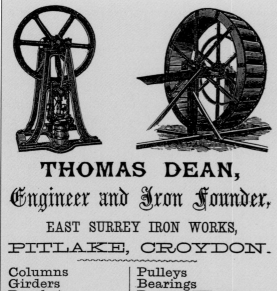

THOMAS DEAN,
Engineer and Iron Founder,
EAST SURREY IRON WORKS,
PITLAKE, CROYDON.

Columns	Pulleys
Girders	Bearings
Brackets	Barrow Wheels
Railings	Furnace Work
Cisterns	Gas Works Castings
Chimney Pieces	Sanitary Castings
Manholes	Stand Pipes
Gulleys	Hydrants
Grates & Frames	Steam Valves
Area Gratings	Steam Cocks
Air Bricks	Force Pumps
Ash Pans	Plank Pumps.

detailed description appears in the *Guide to the South Eastern Railway* of 1858: 'The visitor to Croydon will have an opportunity, as he passes by North End, to inspect the carriage-depot of Messrs. Lenny and Co., one of the most eminent coach-building establishments in the kingdom. Here will be remarked on a large scale, all the preparations requisite to complete the convenient and luxurious carriages, which are unrivalled in Europe … Amongst the multitudinous collection of Broughams, Clarences, Sociables, Phaetons of all kinds in the showrooms, our readers will easily recognise the famous Croydon Basket carriages, which seem to have captivated the public from their first appearance. We are not surprised to hear that these carriages are manufactured in large numbers and sent to all parts of the world.' The company had apparently supplied carriages to the King of Portugal, the King of Sardinia and Queen Victoria.

As in most places, local materials had been used in building for centuries. Locally made bricks were used in building the Whitgift Hospital (1596), and flints, Merstham Stone, and wood were in common use. The great increase in building activity during the 19th century saw the expansion of brick and tile making, gravel digging and chalk quarrying/lime production. In 1875 an unusual industry was developed in South Norwood, possibly in connection with the famous firework displays at Crystal Palace. C.T. Brock and Company opened a firework factory to the south-east of the main railway line at Norwood Junction, in the vicinity of the present Davidson Road. In 1902 the company moved to Sutton. Other local industries included the manufacture of clocks and bells, clay pipes, iron making, a number of laundries, and mineral water and ginger beer factories.

64 (*top left*) *Three examples of Messrs Lenny's Basket Carriages. The Queen's Pattern was described as 'one of the prettiest, and at the same time , most economical … which although patronised by Her Majesty, and some of her wealthiest nobles, may be purchased for eighteen pounds; plain axles, cushions, and shafts included'.*

65 (*left*) *Many of Croydon's older streets still have drain covers bearing the name of the East Surrey Iron Works, Croydon. This advert is from a local street directory.*

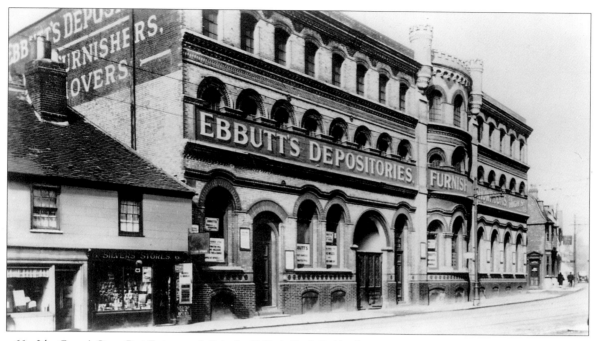

66 *John Cooper's Steam Boot Factory was built in the 1860s in South End by the corner of Lower Coombe Street. After Cooper moved his business to Northampton, the building was used at various times as a newspaper printing works and as a furniture depository, as seen here. At one time Croydon had a number of rather splendid furniture depositories but changing social trends rendered them obsolete. Ebbutt's claimed to be founded in 1718, and eventually became part of Allder's. Although listed, this fine building was replaced by an office block in the 1980s.*

One local man who built up a flourishing industry which later moved away from the area was John Cooper. He was a country shoemaker at West Wickham, retailing his boots and shoes by pony and trap in the Farleigh, Chelsham, Warlingham and West Wickham areas. He later opened a shop in Lower Coombe Street, Croydon. His son, also named John and later to become the second mayor of Croydon, travelled for him and organised the supply of boots on the instalment principle, mostly to agricultural labourers. The business grew and a factory was opened in Lower Coombe Street. In the 1860s bigger premises were opened on the corner of South End and Lower Coombe Street and at the time it was the largest factory in the town. The younger John Cooper acquired a business with premises in London and Northampton in 1876. He also purchased land in Bynes Road, South Croydon on which, between 1878 and 1888, he erected 38 houses and three

shops for his workmen. A great deal of work was 'put out' to the shoemakers living there and the area became known as 'Snob's Island'. With his steam boot manufactory and his 'outdoor working' (very unusual in this part of the country) Cooper was using a combination of new and old methods. In 1894 he closed his Croydon factory and moved to Northampton with about 140 local families.

In the late 1860s the Englishmen's Freehold Land Society was building cottages at what was then called New Thornton Heath. The station had opened with the Balham and Croydon railway line in 1862. Societies such as this were formed by politicians whose aim was to encourage thrift in the working classes by providing them with the opportunity to purchase a home and, in consequence, giving them the vote. The largest estate under development in the 1870s was at Park Hill. It was laid out by the Ecclesiastical Commissioners in 1861. The houses were large, leasehold and very

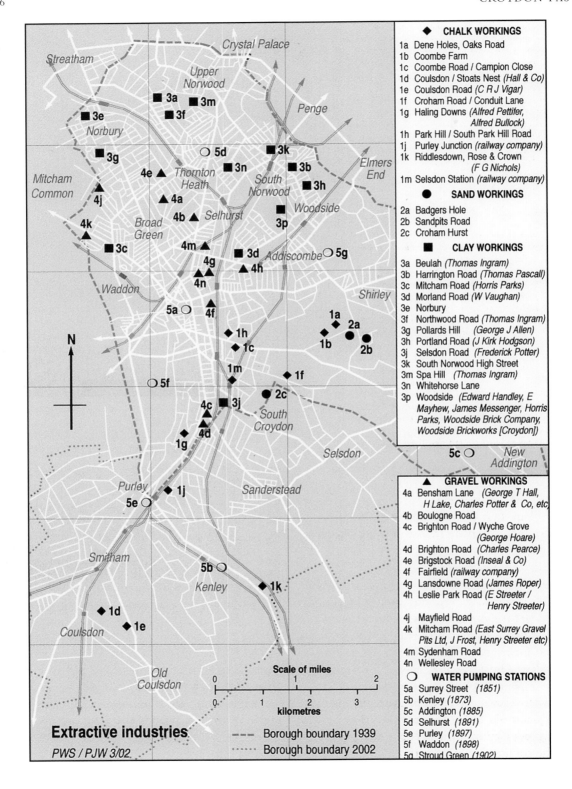

◆ **CHALK WORKINGS**
1a Dene Holes, Oaks Road
1b Coombe Farm
1c Coombe Road / Campion Close
1d Coulsdon / Stoats Nest *(Hall & Co)*
1e Coulsdon Road *(C R J Vigar)*
1f Croham Road / Conduit Lane
1g Haling Downs *(Alfred Pettifer,*
   Alfred Bullock)
1h Park Hill / South Park Hill Road
1j Purley Junction *(railway company)*
1k Riddlesdown, Rose & Crown
   (F G Nichols)
1m Selsdon Station *(railway company)*

● **SAND WORKINGS**
2a Badgers Hole
2b Sandpits Road
2c Croham Hurst

■ **CLAY WORKINGS**
3a Beulah *(Thomas Ingram)*
3b Harrington Road *(Thomas Pascall)*
3c Mitcham Road *(Horris Parks)*
3d Morland Road *(W Vaughan)*
3e Norbury
3f Northwood Road *(Thomas Ingram)*
3g Pollards Hill   *(George J Allen)*
3h Portland Road *(J Kirk Hodgson)*
3j Selsdon Road *(Frederick Potter)*
3k South Norwood High Street
3m Spa Hill   *(Thomas Ingram)*
3n Whitehorse Lane
3p Woodside *(Edward Handley, E*
   Mayhew, James Messenger, Horris
   Parks, Woodside Brick Company,
   Woodside Brickworks [Croydon])

▲ **GRAVEL WORKINGS**
4a Bensham Lane *(George T Hall,*
   H Lake, Charles Potter & Co, etc)
4b Boulogne Road
4c Brighton Road / Wyche Grove
   (George Hoare)
4d Brighton Road *(Charles Pearce)*
4e Brigstock Road *(Inseal & Co)*
4f Fairfield *(railway company)*
4g Lansdowne Road *(James Roper)*
4h Leslie Park Road *(E Streeter /*
   Henry Streeter)
4j Mayfield Road
4k Mitcham Road *(East Surrey Gravel*
   Pits Ltd, J Frost, Henry Streeter etc)
4m Sydenham Road
4n Wellesley Road

○ **WATER PUMPING STATIONS**
5a Surrey Street *(1851)*
5b Kenley *(1873)*
5c Addington *(1885)*
5d Selhurst *(1891)*
5e Purley *(1897)*
5f Waddon *(1898)*
5g Stroud Green *(1902)*

Extractive industries

PWS / PJW 3/02

Scale of miles
0   1   2

0   1   2   3
kilometres

– – – Borough boundary 1939
· · · · · Borough boundary 2002

67 *(facing page)   This map shows the approximate locations of the more important chalk, sand, clay and gravel pits, and public supply wells in the borough. They are mostly of 19th- and 20th-century date. The distribution of the pits obviously reflects the underlying geology. All the wells remain in use but there are no longer active pits in the locality.*

Local materials were used almost exclusively in building until the 20th century. Many houses were of wood, and later flints. Bricks, which had been made locally for at least four hundred years, were made at Park Hill and Duppas Hill during the construction of the Whitgift Hospital. The London Clay of north Croydon was freely available for brick, tile and pottery manufacture until recent years, the large Woodside Brickworks only ceasing production in 1974.

68 *(top right)   This 1866 photograph shows Thomas Pascall's Brick Field and Pottery at South Norwood. It was sited between South Norwood Hill and the High Street, partly in the grounds now occupied by Cumberlow Lodge behind the Stanley Halls. (3k on map – facing page.)*

69 *(right)   Chalk was used for lime burning for agricultural and building purposes, including road and railway embankments. The largest industrial-scale limeworks active in the 19th and 20th century were at Coulsdon, Haling Downs and Riddlesdown. This postcard view shows Haling Chalk Pit and Biddulph Road at Purley Oaks around 1910. The works here ceased production early in the 20th century and the chalk face is now barely visible through the undergrowth. (1g on map – facing page.)*

70 *(below right)   Croydon gravel was famous during the 19th century and Ordnance Survey maps of the period show extensive gravel pits all around the town. Most of the Fair Field was excavated and this photograph shows gravel being dug at a pit in Lansdowne Road behind Wellesley Road around 1910. (4g on map – facing page.)*

expensive and did not go very well at first; some of those in Park Hill Road could only draw water in the mornings, when the reservoir was full after a night's pumping, as the houses were sited above the supply. Francis Moore, who lived at no.1 Park Hill Rise, wrote in the *Croydon Chronicle*, 'Ours was the first house built in the rise in 1868, although Mr Henry Hart had six others in course of erection. One could frequently hear the nightingale in those days and I once surprised a covey of partridges in my garden.' The rural seclusion of Croydon was attracting people to migrate from London to a place where they could enjoy pleasant surroundings and a quaint old town. To serve the needs of the growing population, many people also moved in from the countryside to the south and further away,

seizing the opportunities to escape from the drudgery, uncertainties and squalor of work as an agricultural labourer. They took work in the building trade, local factories or in domestic service.

As early as 1862 the magazine *London Society* said of Croydon, 'Handsome villas spring up on every side tenanted by City men whose portly persons crowd the trains.' In *The Railway in Town and Country 1830-1914*, Professor Jack Simmons wrote,

> By 1865 Croydon had grown into the centre of a complicated railway system … There was no mistaking Croydon's character by that time. It had become a dormitory town. But unlike most dormitories it was also a town in the full sense of the word. It was urban and suburban at once … By the 1880s there were well over 100 trains to London every week-day.

Until the 1850s Croydon did not have its own local newspaper but had to be content with local news contained in the *Surrey Standard*, or the *Maidstone and South Eastern Gazette*. A somewhat scurrilous journal had appeared for a short while in the 1830s, but the stamp duties deterred publication of a reasonable paper until they were finally abolished in 1855. That year marked the publication of the *Croydon Chronicle* by Frederick Baldiston. In 1861 the *Croydon Times* appeared for the first time and this was soon followed by the *Croydon Journal* and *Croydon Observer*, both published in Lewes from

1863 until about 1904. In 1869 Jesse Ward started to publish the *Croydon Advertiser*, which remained a family business into the 1980s; it is still published but is now part of a large group. These papers were soon followed by others such as the *Croydon Guardian* and *Croydon Express*, which survived until about 1916. There were numerous others in the late 19th and early 20th centuries, most of which had very short lives; these included daily and evening papers such as the *Croydon Daily Argus* and *Surrey Evening Echo*.

Having dealt with water supply and drainage, the Local Board of Health built municipal slaughter-houses (which continued in use until 1955), provided public baths, acquired recreation grounds and open spaces (for example, Duppas Hill in 1865 and part of Addington Hills in 1874), formed a fire brigade and developed an innovative farm irrigation scheme for the treatment of sewage. However, there was increasing conflict over what it did (spent too much money) and what it did not do (widen the narrow High Street).

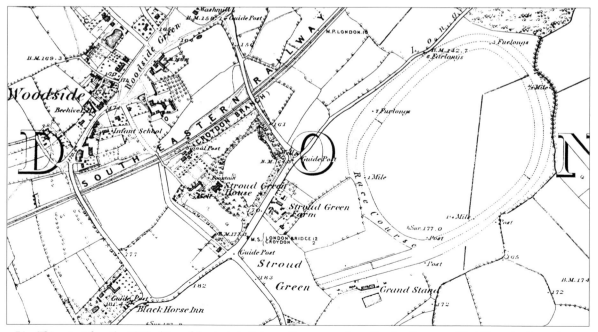

71   *This extract from the 1868 edition of the six-inch Ordnance Survey map shows Croydon Racecourse. Woodside station is not shown, presumably because it opened after the survey for the map.*

72 The International Hurdle Race at Croydon.

A move for incorporation as a borough was successful and in 1883 the charter was borne through the town with much ceremony. The new borough boundaries followed almost exactly those of the old parish, but Selsdon (Croydon Crook) was added to Sanderstead. The newly formed council took over all the powers of the Local Board of Health but had wider compulsory powers which were strengthened in 1889 when the town was given county borough status. This meant it had the full powers of a county, which it retained until 1965 local government reorganisation.

More railway lines had opened and small clusters of development started to grow up near the new stations. A group of local businessmen formed the Croydon Tramways Company and in 1879 the first of several horse-drawn tramway lines opened. The trams provided the first regular local public transport services in the town and also brought improved road surfaces.

Croydon Fair continued to attract large crowds into the 1850s and '60s but there was growing local opposition to it because of the unruly crowds it attracted. The railway had made it much easier for people from afar to attend. It was suppressed in 1867–8 and crowds attacked the police station and smashed the windows of magistrates' houses in revenge. In fact, the threat of riot and disorder was never far away. Local celebrations of Guy Fawkes night often resulted in pitched battles with the police in the town centre.

Horse racing seems to have taken place in Croydon from the Middle Ages onwards and Queen Elizabeth I visited a race meeting here in 1585. A straight racecourse along the Brighton Road is shown on early maps. Steeplechase meetings were held at Selhurst in 1858 and 1859 which were a success and in 1860 the races moved to Park Hill. In 1866 the land was sold for building development and a site at Stroud Green was obtained on a 14-year lease. The railway station at Woodside was opened in 1871, complete with a ramp for the horses, to serve the racecourse which became increasingly popular, attracting many racegoers from London. Valuable races such as the Great Metropolitan became well established as major Grand National trials, and by 1876 Croydon had 17 fixtures a year.

From 1879 it was necessary to have a licence to operate a racecourse. In 1883 the newly elected Borough Council had to comment on renewal of the licence. There was some opposition because of the undesirable people racing attracted to the locality. Councillor Hinton referred to the way in which Woodside racecourse blighted the vicinity, deterring new building. He asked for support 'to put an end to the blasting, blighting and withering influence that the races spread all around … If you think I exaggerate, go and taste the pestilential air that is belched forth from thousands of throats in filthy conversation.' He asked the mayor 'to purge this fair borough from this terrible and pernicious influence … and to remove this foul blot, which like a festering canker, was eating out the vitals of their moral system.' Another councillor thought they should not interfere on moral grounds and would be wrong to stop the races 'while they allowed and gave police protection to a gang of roughs who went through the town with a band' (referring to the Salvation Army). There was continued opposition to the races on a variety of grounds and when Croydon became a county borough it gained the authority to issue licences. The Licensing Committee refused to renew the licence and the last

73 *The Friends School in Park Lane, 1858. After the school moved to Saffron Walden in 1879 the wings seen here were demolished. The central building later became St Anselm's School. It was one of the finest 18th-century buildings in the town but was sadly destroyed by a land mine in the Second World War. Taberner House now stands on the site.*

74 *Addington National School was opened in 1844. Photographed on 5 May 1870, it was Croydon's last village school and closed in 1950. It was used as the parish hall for some years, but was demolished in 1967.*

75 The Mitre *public house in Canterbury Road is on the left of this photograph showing ploughing at Waddon Marsh Farm in 1884. Wildbore's Lane ran alongside the public house. Farmland remained in many parts of the town throughout the Victorian period and well into the 20th century, and the new suburban residents co-existed with country activities.*

76 This 1887 advertisement presumably survived because of pigs being found dead at the Wildbores! The name actually derives from Daniel Wildbore, who owned the land around here in the 1850s.

CORPORATION OF CROYDON

£2 REWARD.

The above Reward will be paid for correct information as to the Name and Address of the OWNER OF SIX PIGS, that were found dead on the 21st January, 1887, in a Field at "The Wildbores," Canterbury Road.

Information to be given to Mr. R. A. THRALE, the Veterinary Inspector the Borough, No. 68, George Street, Croydon.

10th February, 1887.

C. M. ELBOROUGH
Town

JESSE W. WARD, STEAM PRINTER, KATHARINE STREET, CROYDON.

races were at the National Hunt meeting in November 1890. The course management bought a site at Gatwick and the races were transferred there in 1891. The Croydon Hurdle and Metropolitan Steeplechase meetings were still run and racing continued at Gatwick until 1940.

Other opportunities for leisure were increasing during the period. In 1838 the Croydon Literary and Scientific Institution had been formed. It met in the former theatre on Crown Hill but in 1860 moved to the newly erected Public Halls in George Street, which were the home for concerts, exhibitions and meetings of all types until the 1950s. Class distinction was very much a fact of life. The Croydon Workmen's Club was set up in 1864 and became by 1886 the Central Croydon Liberal and Working Men's Club. The Croydon Microscopical Club was formed in 1870, and by 1902 had taken on the broader title of the Croydon Natural History and Scientific Society. It flourishes still and has an unbroken record of publishing over more than 130 years. Croydon Camera Club was founded in 1891 and it too continues its work into the 21st century. Many other organisations provided for a variety of sports, musical and social activities but most of them were founded by men, run by men and existed for men until well into the 20th century.

The Victorians took their pleasures very seriously. For sheer stamina it would be hard to beat the 150 ladies and gentlemen of the Surrey Archaeological Society on their annual excursion on 7 August 1875. They set off at 11a.m. in 'vehicles of all descriptions for Sanderstead and Sanderstead Court' where two papers were read. They then proceeded to Warlingham church, where another paper was read. Refreshments followed in a tent erected on Warlingham Green, after which the company went on to visit Farleigh church, and then to Wickham Court, where they were shown over the house and grounds, and listened to another paper. Tea, coffee and light refreshments were provided and the party then continued to West Wickham

church, listened to a further paper, and then went on to Addington church for another two papers.

By then it was 6p.m., an hour after the party was due back in Croydon, but they did not give up and walked through Addington Park, where they met the Archbishop and inspected the house. Arriving back in Croydon, they sat down in the Public Hall to 'an excellent cold collation … prepared by Mr Thomas Green of the Crown'. This was followed by six toasts, with appropriate speeches and a vote of thanks. Presumably those members of the society who came from distant parts of the county, such as Farnham and Guildford, then set off on their long journey home!

The social structure of the town changed considerably as the century went on. In his excellent book, *Religion and Urban Change – Croydon 1840-1914*, Jeremy Morris argues that the town probably reached its peak of affluence in the 1860s and then began to decline. It was a town dominated by Anglicanism in the first half of the Victorian period but its religious affiliations were broadly in

77 *(above)   Blunt House stood in South End between where Aberdeen and Ledbury Roads now enter it. It dated from the mid-18th century and some years after the Blunt family left it was leased by William Coles, who Garrow said in 1818 'made such tasteful additions to the buildings and pleasure grounds, as not only to adorn the estate, but also considerably improve the Southern approach to the town of Croydon'. The last two occupants were the celebrated architect, Sir Gilbert Scott, and his son, John Oldrid Scott. The house was pulled down around 1889.*

78 *(facing page, top)   Coombe Hill House stands on the corner of Coombe Road and Park Lane. Dating from the early 18th century, it is an imposing example of a Georgian town house. From about 1851 until 1880 it was owned by Robert Amadeus, Baron Heath, seen here (left) relaxing in the grounds in 1879. He was Italian Consul General in London, a director of the Royal Exchange Assurance Corporation, and chairman of the Sao Paulo Railway. Locally he was a great supporter of the Whitgift Foundation of which he was a governor from 1855 to 1882. He actively concerned himself in the affairs of Shirley parish. In 1880 he moved to Coombe House, died in 1882, and was buried in Shirley churchyard. Coombe Hill House became a preparatory school around 1930, and was bought by the Labour Party in 1966. As Ruskin House it is now their headquarters in Croydon.*

79 *(facing page, bottom)   In contrast to the grandeur of Coombe Hill House, in 1889 these cottages were only a few yards away down Coombe Road near the corner of the High Street. The Victorian houses in the background were opposite Coombe Hill House and fairly new at this time.*

80   Scenes such as this were commonplace between the 1850s and 1930s. A new road is being laid out in the fields at Woodside in about 1896. It would become Sonning Road but the first new houses were not built until 1902.

81   West Street was laid out in the 1840s and has a good selection of styles of small Victorian terraced houses, dating from the 1840s onwards, as well as the Providence Strict Baptist Chapel of 1847 (right). St Andrew's Church (1857), originally known as the 'church in the meadow', forms a landmark at the end. A block of 1960s flats in the distance brings a touch of modernity to the scene.

line with London as a whole by the early 1900s. Incorporation offered Liberal nonconformists an opportunity to bring about improvements that had been resisted by the formerly conservative, largely Anglican, domination. No longer was the church the force it had been in local matters and increasingly local businessmen had the affairs of the town in their hands.

Several schemes put forward by the new borough council foundered due to lack of support. These included a proposal to establish a Free Library, a Jubilee Fund intended to purchase the old archiepiscopal palace for the town and, most important, the widening of the narrow High Street. The main problem was the two main factions in the town:

82   This 1888 photograph of a cottage in Coulsdon Street shows a simple rural home of the late Victorian period. Many of the country folk in the Croydon area would have lived in similar style. The paint on the walls is peeling, the floor is of stone and appears to have grass growing in the gaps. The smock hanging in the large open fireplace indicates that the occupant worked on the land.

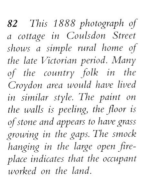

83 (top) In 1860 North End consisted mainly of private houses, with only a few shops. The Rising Sun *public house is on the left in the distance.*

84 (bottom) Thirty years later this photograph from virtually the same viewpoint shows the conversion of nearly all the buildings to commercial use. The road surface has been partly paved by the tramway company, but the gas lamp on the right remains and the inn sign of the Rising Sun *can still be seen in the distance.*

85   *Croydon High Street in 1893 still retained its old-fashioned appearance, with the inn sign of the Greyhound stretching across the road. The bow-windowed building on the right was formerly the* Red Lion *inn which closed around 1800. It was demolished in the 1920s. The buildings on the left were all removed so that the street could be widened, and those on the right went in the 1960s. St George's Walk now occupies the site.*

86   *Jabez Spencer Balfour was born in 1843. For years he was the most popular man in Croydon. When he first came to the town he lived in London Road, and later at Wellesley House, which stood approximately where the Wellesley Road multi-storey car park is today. He took an interest in practically every movement in the town and was natural choice for Charter Mayor in 1883. He was at that time Liberal MP for Tamworth, and later became MP for Burnley. As a young man he had shown a genius for speculation and became associated with a group of companies of which the Liberator Building Society was the principal one. In September 1892 this failed and Balfour fled to South America. Eventually he was arrested there, extradited, and sentenced to 14 years' hard labour. Many thousands of small savers lost their life savings. He died in 1916.*

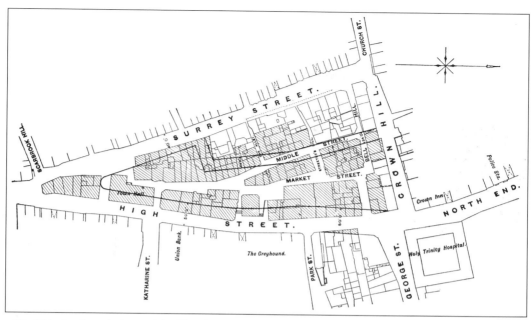

87   *This plan shows the layout of the old market area with the proposed Improvement Scheme new roads and widened High Street indicated by solid black lines.*

88   *Surrey Street was formerly known as Butcher Row. This view from the High Street corner shows it before the market area was redeveloped in the 1890s. The Old Kings Head on the right was at one time kept by a relative of John Ruskin, who in 1885 wrote '… it is evident to me in retrospect … that the personal feeling and native instinct of me had been fastened irrevocably long before to things modest, humble and pure in peace, under the low red roofs of Croydon, and by the cress set rivulets in which the sand danced and minnows darted above the springs of Wandel'. The Three Tuns on the left was a well-known local hostelry, with a bowling green. The building beyond is the Old Jail, built by public subscription in 1803. It was demolished in the late 1950s.*

89 (above)   This view of Market Street in about 1890 shows some of the interesting buildings in the area. They would have been an asset to the town if they had not become so dilapidated.

these were the tradespeople in the town centre, who favoured improvement and the use of public funds to that end; and the tradesmen in South and Upper Norwood and Thornton Heath, who were suspicious of town centre improvements which would attract shoppers, allied with the new residents who worked in London, enjoyed the quaint country atmosphere of Croydon and did not want its old–fashioned appearance changed.

However the town centre problems could not be ignored. The triangle formed by High Street, Crown Hill and Surrey Street had been at one time an open space, typical of market places in many towns such as East Grinstead and Bletchingley. Gradually the temporary stalls were replaced by permanent structures, but by the mid-19th century the area had become run down. It contained a

90 (right)   Central Croydon station was opened in 1868 in the newly constructed Katharine Street. The terminus of a short branch line from East Croydon, it was not very successful and was open for only a few years. The Corporation bought the site for its new Town Hall and laid out gardens in the former railway cutting. Sidings remained on Fairfield until the mid-1930s. The Croydon Farmers Club was established by 1858. Another local organisation with farming interests was the East Surrey Agricultural Association, which was formed in 1837.

CROYDON FARMERS' CLUB
FAT STOCK,
CORN AND ROOT
→⊱ SHOW ⊰←

WILL BE HELD AT THE

Croydon Central Station,

KATHARINE STREET,

ON

Thursday, December 11, 1884.

The Show will be Open to the Public at Twelve o'clock.

CLOSE AT TEN P.M.

Admission 1/- ; after Five o'clock, 6d.

91 *The new Town Hall was opened by the Prince of Wales on 19 May 1896. The 176-foot high clock tower has been a notable landmark ever since and symbolises the town for many Croydonians.*

92 Joshua Allder was born at Walworth in 1838 and opened a small draper's shop in North End when he was about thirty. He soon established a good reputation and expanded his business into adjacent premises. In 1894 he expanded the shop further into George Street, by which time it occupied nearly an acre. He was one of the founders of West Croydon Baptist Chapel (Spurgeon's Tabernacle). A Liberal, he was elected to the Local Board of Health in 1881, and later won a seat on the Council. He was known for his quiet acts of kindness to the poor, especially in Middle Row. He died in 1904. His son carried on the business but died young and the store became part of the Holdron group.

93 Wandle Park was laid out on Stubb's Mead and Frog's Mead, low-lying land through which the River Wandle flowed. Artificial lakes were created and the park was opened in May 1890 by the mayor. It was reported that 'something like 30,000 people promenaded the new park … The majority of these gathered round the borders of the lake, where boating was in progress, and where the proceedings were from time to time enlivened by the precipitation into the water of sundry grave and reverend personages who ought to have known better.' A lowering of the water table led to the filling in of the lakes in the 1960s.

94 *This old farmhouse was in Thornton Heath on the corner of Parchmore and Brigstock Roads, where Tesco's supermarket stands in 2002. It was formerly Colliers Water, or Walker's Green Farm. Note the use of flints in the construction of the wall. Many legends concern this farm, some involving charcoal burners. Later it was believed to have been the haunt of highwaymen and footpads, as the building had a secret staircase into the roof. The farm buildings were demolished around 1899.*

95 *This photograph was taken in October 1894 at Croydon Cattle Fair. The first day was devoted to cattle and sheep, and the second to horses and ponies, when it was attended by the lower classes, gypsies, costers and copers. The drovers would arrive before daylight with their sheep, covered with rime on a frosty morning, and the booth keepers did a good trade supplying them with breakfast of boiled beef, beer and coffee. The man on the left wearing a smock was probably a drover or carter. In the background are the* Purley Arms *public house and houses on the east side of Brighton Road. This field succumbed to the house builder the following year and Churchill Road now occupies the land.*

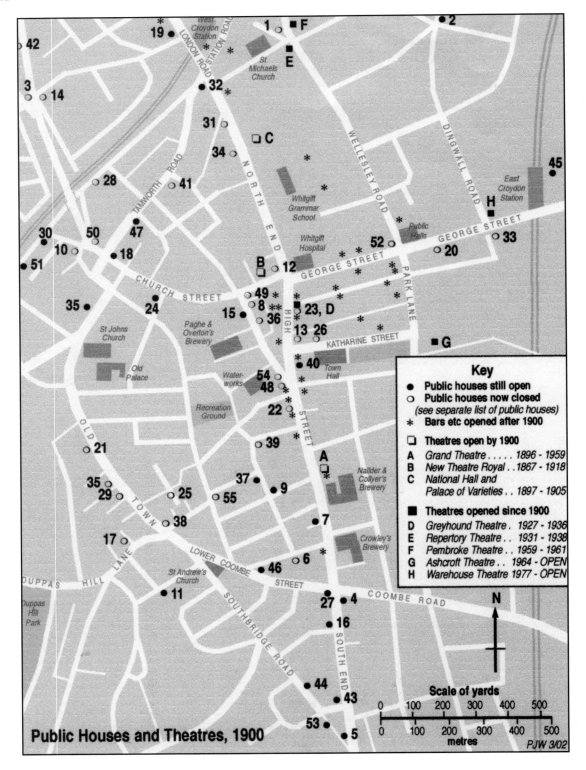

Key

● Public houses still open
○ Public houses now closed
(see separate list of public houses)
* Bars etc opened after 1900

❏ Theatres open by 1900
A Grand Theatre . . . . . 1896 - 1959
B New Theatre Royal . . 1867 - 1918
C National Hall and
   Palace of Varieties . . 1897 - 1905

■ Theatres opened since 1900
D Greyhound Theatre . 1927 - 1936
E Repertory Theatre . . 1931 - 1938
F Pembroke Theatre . . 1959 - 1961
G Ashcroft Theatre . . 1964 - OPEN
H Warehouse Theatre 1977 - OPEN

Scale of yards

Public Houses and Theatres, 1900

PJW 3/02

network of narrow streets and alleys and between 1851 and 1861 the population within the triangle increased from 449 to 590. Many of the houses were lodging houses, containing an average of 24 persons, some of the women being prostitutes. In 1888 the *Croydon Chronicle* described some of the lodging houses as 'A human moral piggery that, for low depravity, either Newcastle or Manchester might match, but certainly could not surpass'.

Soon after incorporation in 1883 the council appointed a High Street Improvement Committee, but it took many years of heated discussion and

96 (facing page)   This map of the town centre shows the position of public houses and theatres existing in 1900. The key is given below.

97 (right)   On 12 July 1897 large crowds turned out to welcome the Colonial Troops who were guests of the nation for Queen Victoria's Diamond Jubilee. The troops marched from West Croydon station to the Grand Theatre and are seen here in North End passing Tamworth Road (left). The procession includes detachments of the Victoria Mounted Rifles, the Canadian North West Mounted Military Police, the New Zealand Mounted Rifles, the Borneo Military Police, the Natal Mounted Rifles and the New South Wales Lancers.

Key to map of public houses in Central Croydon
Arranged in alphabetical order

1	ALHAMBRA, Wellesley Road	1872 - 1978
2	BEDFORD ARMS, Sydenham Road	1853 - OPEN
3	BLACK BOY, Mitcham Road	1855 - 1967
4	BLACKSMITH'S ARMS, South End	1853 - OPEN
5	BLUE ANCHOR, South End	1644 - OPEN
6	BREWERS ARMS, West Street	1864 - 1907
7	BRICKLAYERS ARMS, High Street	1750? - 1929
8	BRITANNIA, Surrey Street	1637? - 1939
9	BULLS HEAD, Laud Street	1864 - OPEN
10	COACH & HORSES, Lower Church St	1869 - 1969
11	CRICKETERS, Southbridge Place	1850 - OPEN
12	CROWN, North End	1443? - 1950?
13	CROYDON, High Street	1900 - 1965
14	DERBY ARMS, Pitlake	1832 - OPEN
15	DOG & BULL, Surrey Street	1595? - OPEN
16	DUKES HEAD, South End	1761 - OPEN
17	DUPPAS HILL HOTEL, Duppas Hill	1849 - 1922
18	EAGLE, Lower Church Street	1865 - OPEN
19	FOX & HOUNDS, London Road	1843 - OPEN
20	GEORGE IV, George Street	1843 - 1958
21	GLOBE, Old Town	1843 - 1960?
22	GREEN DRAGON, High Street	1668 - 1960?
23	GREYHOUND, High Street	1493 - 1959
24	GUN, Church Street	1746? - OPEN
25	JOLLY BLEACHERS, Union Street	1843 -1906
26	KINGS ARMS, Katharine Street	1845 - 1961
27	NEW INN, South End	1838? - 1929
28	ODDFELLOWS ARMS, Waddon New Rd	1864 - 1955
29	OLD GEORGE, Old Town	1832? - 1968?
30	PITLAKE, Waddon New Rd	1864 - OPEN
31	RAILWAY ARMS, North End	1843 - 1956
32	RAILWAY BELL, North End	1851 - OPEN
33	RAILWAY HOTEL, George Street	1841 - 1980
34	RISING SUN, North End	1665? - 1951
35	ROSE & CROWN, Church Street	1680? - OPEN
36	ROYAL OAK, Surrey Street	1700? - 1965?
37	ROYAL STANDARD, Sheldon Street	1869 - OPEN
38	RUNNING HORSE, Old Town	1780? - 1961
39	SHELDON ARMS, Whitgift Street	1869 - 1955?
40	SHIP, High Street	1640 - OPEN
41	SIR ROBERT PEEL, Tamworth Road	1869 - 1963
42	SIX BELLS, Handcroft Road	1855 - 1967
43	SOUTHBRIDGE ARMS, South End	1869 - 1927
44	STAR, Southbridge Road	1859 - OPEN
45	STATION HOTEL, Station Yard	1869 - OPEN
46	SURREY CRICKETERS, West Street	1853 - OPEN
47	TAMWORTH ARMS, Tamworth Road	1855 - OPEN
48	THREE TUNS, Surrey Street	1651 - 1906
49	VICTORY, Crown Hill	1867 - 1934
50	VOLUNTEER, Pitlake	1810 - 1970
51	WANDLE ARMS, Waddon New Road	1865 - OPEN
52	WELLINGTON, George Street	1869 - 1914
53	WHEELWRIGHTS, Southbridge Road	1882 - OPEN
54	WHITE HART, Surrey Street	1855 - 1921
55	WHITGIFT ARMS, Church Road	1861 - 1960?

98 *The Grand Theatre and Opera House was opened in 1896 by Herbert Beerbohm Tree. It stood in the High Street, opposite Whitgift Street, and was closed and demolished in 1959. Grosvenor House occupies the site. This photograph is thought to show an outing for staff and possibly performers.*

99 *There were two other theatres in the town at the end of the 19th century. Rather confusingly, the Crown Hill theatre had become the Empire by 1897, the name later adopted by the North End theatre. These advertisements give a flavour of the type of entertainment on offer in the 1890s when many people regarded theatres as dens of iniquity.*

National Palace
THEATRE OF VARIETIES.
NORTH END, CROYDON.

Lessees ... ... The National Palace of Varieties, Ltd.
General Manager ... ... Mr. J. SPARROW.
Resident Manager ... ... Mr. P. A. LENNON.
Secretary .. .. Mr. G. E. S. VENNER.
Telephone No. 174 Croydon. Telegraphic Address: "Palace," Croydon.

OPEN EVERY EVENING.
MONDAY, DEC. 6th, 1897,
And Every Evening during the week.

HARRY RANDALL The Great Comic Vocalist and Comedian.

Mdlle. LALO The Beautiful Electric Bicyclist.

RUMBO AUSTIN and his Comical Four NIPPERS.

SARINA The White Demon.

ADA CERITO Serio-Comedienne and Elegant Dancer

R. H. DOUGLASS in his Original Monologue, "The Comic Opera Rehearsal.

AMY HORTON The Australian Burlesque Actress.

The Brothers ARTHUR Instrumentalists, and Song and Dance Artistes

EVALO & Co. The Three Tricky Turks.

The BROWN & KELLY Combination
In a Screamingly Funny Sketch,

Doors Open at 7.30. Commence at 7.45. On Saturdays Early Doors Open at 6.45, 3d. extra to all parts.
PRICES—3s., 2s., 1s. 6d., 1s., and 6d.
HALF PRICE to all Parts Gallery excepted, at nine o'clock.

THE EMPIRE
THEATRE OF VARIETIES
CROWN HILL, CROYDON.

Joint Managing Directors .. Mr. FRED BARTLETT & Mr. EDMUND G. PRATT.

MONDAY, DEC. 6th, 1897, and Every Evening.
First Appearance in Croydon of
JAMES BERRY,
Late PUBLIC EXECUTIONER,
In his interesting LECTURE and DIORAMA of "ENGLAND'S PRISONS AND PRISONERS."
Berry has assisted at 500 executions, and has himself hanged 193 people.

The SISTERS ASHER (ROSE and AGNES),
Dainty Comediennes, Vocalists & Dancers.

CHARLES PAVER, Character Vocal Comedian.

The GARDEN MELVIN QUINTETTE,
International Dancers and Pipers.

The Three SISTERS LYRIC, "Les Militaires" Trio.

F. V. ST. CLAIR, The Great Topical Singer and Author.

MARIE VENTON, Fascinating Serio and Dancer.

CLOWN DIDIE GODFREY and his Marvellous TROUPE OF DOGS.

Mdlle. NAOMI ETHARDO, Contortionist, Juggler, and Hand-Balancer.

TINY ARNOLD, The Smallest Burlesque Artiste in the World.

DRISCOLL & BEATTIE COMBINATION
In their Terrific Screamer, entitled "McFEE, M.P."

MATINEE, SATURDAY at 2.30.
Doors Open at 7. Commence at 7.30. Carriages 10.45.
Grand Circle and Stalls, 2s.; Pit Stalls, 1s.; Pit, 9d.; Gallery, 6d. Seats in Private Boxes, 3s. each.
Second Price at 9 o'clock (Gallery excepted): Grand Circle and Stalls, 1s., Pit Stalls and Pit 6d.; Seats in Private Boxes, 1s. 6d.
To avoid the crowd Early Door will be opened at 6.40. 3d. extra to all parts

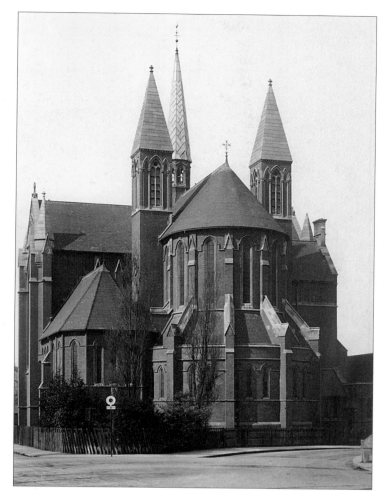

100 *A new parish of St Michael's was established in 1871. After using some old stables, worshippers brought a temporary wooden church from Folkestone, and in 1881 the splendid new church in Poplar Walk was opened. Designed by the noted architect of Truro Cathedral, John Loughborough Pearson, it is Croydon's finest Victorian church. Originally it was intended to include a high tower, but insufficient funds were available.*

Corporation acquired the site for a new Town Hall, with space for a police station and a sunken garden in the railway cutting. The council had to give up the ancient public footpath that ran diagonally from near the George Street/Park Lane junction across Fairfield to Park Hill. This angered the influential Park Hill residents but the scheme went ahead and demolition started in 1893. The council were required to build ten cottages in Mint Walk to house some of the dispossessed residents, and to provide a hostel for temporary residents, which was built in Pitlake.

The new Town Hall buildings included a public library (to replace one that had been provided in a North End shop in 1890), a fine reference library (the Braithwaite Hall, named after the former vicar who had died suddenly, and whose daughter later became Dame Lilian Braithwaite), and a Corn Exchange, which is a reminder of the continuing importance of agriculture in the town's economy. The Town Hall was opened by the Prince of Wales on 19 May 1896. It was regarded by many at the time as an example of gross municipal extravagance. Now known as the Clocktower, it includes a new library, museum and galleries, and the small David Lean Cinema as well as the beautifully restored Council Chamber and Committee Rooms.

argument before any real progress was made. Following a town poll which showed a large majority in favour of improvement, parliamentary powers were sought and the Croydon Improvement Act eventually received Royal Assent in July 1890. This gave the Corporation the right to purchase land in the triangle compulsorily, and then to lease, sell or exchange it. Fortuitously the Brighton Railway Company wanted to dispose of its central station in Katharine Street. A deal was arranged by which the

In 1896 the Corporation opened its new electric power station and introduced the first electric street lights in the town centre. Croydon was well placed to enter another period of growth and progress in the new century.

101 *(overleaf)* *This map shows the location of churches and chapels in the town centre in 1900.*

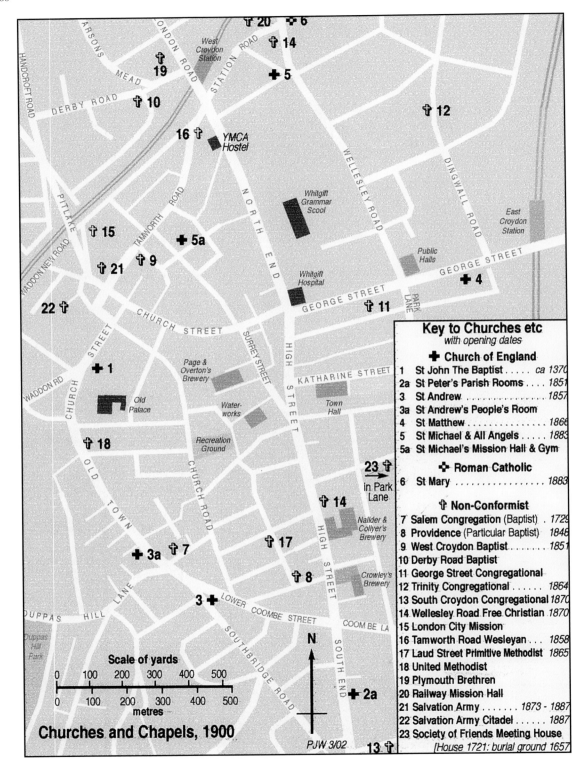

Churches and Chapels, 1900

Scale of yards

0 100 200 300 400 500

0 100 200 300 400 500
metres

N

PJW 3/02

Key to Churches etc
with opening dates

✚ **Church of England**

1	St John The Baptist	ca 1370
2a	St Peter's Parish Rooms	1851
3	St Andrew	1857
3a	St Andrew's People's Room	
4	St Matthew	1866
5	St Michael & All Angels	1883
5a	St Michael's Mission Hall & Gym	

✢ **Roman Catholic**

6	St Mary	1883

✟ **Non-Conformist**

7	Salem Congregation (Baptist)	1729
8	Providence (Particular Baptist)	1848
9	West Croydon Baptist	1851
10	Derby Road Baptist	
11	George Street Congregational	
12	Trinity Congregational	1864
13	South Croydon Congregational	1870
14	Wellesley Road Free Christian	1870
15	London City Mission	
16	Tamworth Road Wesleyan	1858
17	Laud Street Primitive Methodist	1865
18	United Methodist	
19	Plymouth Brethren	
20	Railway Mission Hall	
21	Salvation Army	1873 - 1887
22	Salvation Army Citadel	1887
23	Society of Friends Meeting House	

[House 1721: burial ground 1657

VII

Countryside in Retreat 1901-1951

QUEEN VICTORIA died on 22 January 1901. She had been on the throne since 1837 and during that time Croydon had seen its population increase ninefold and had changed out of all recognition. The next half century would see almost another doubling in population, two major world wars and perhaps even greater changes in lifestyle than hitherto.

There was still plenty of open countryside within Croydon's borders and around, and the town continued to function as the agricultural centre for East Surrey. But its character changed dramatically as it became increasingly a residence for London commuters. Addington and Shirley remained largely rural, and the villages of Coulsdon and Sanderstead away from the railways were remote settlements on

102 *Purley station was opened in 1841 as Godstone Road, but closed in 1847 as the area was almost completely devoid of population. It reopened as Caterham Junction in 1856 when the branch line was laid along the Caterham Valley. It was renamed Purley in 1881 and had just been rebuilt when this photograph was taken in about 1900. A few houses had been built in Foxley Lane (centre) but otherwise open, rolling downland was the main feature of the landscape.*

the downs, virtually untouched by urban development, but this would change over the next 35 years as the introduction of the electric tram, the motor vehicle and motor bus services made it easier to travel greater distances from the railway stations.

The town had 21 separate parishes with their churches, and there were some 60 nonconformist churches, chapels and meeting rooms. Along the main road through the town the horse tramway tracks were being torn up and replaced by those for the new electric trams, the first route being opened between the borough boundaries at Norbury and Purley on 26 September 1901. Others soon followed and new shopping centres soon grew

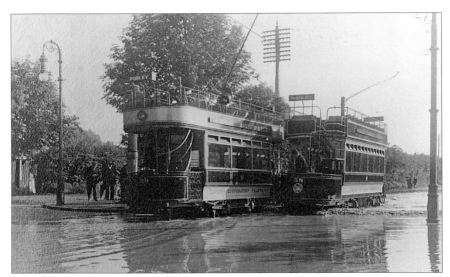

103   Croydon's electric tramways opened between 1901 and 1906. In 1904 there was a particularly severe outbreak of the Bourne and this photograph was taken in Brighton Road at Purley, which still had a rural appearance although building was proceeding rapidly.

104   These fine gates stand at the entrance to Rose Walk on the Webb estate at Purley. In the Edwardian period hundreds of Croydonians would travel out to Purley by tram on Sundays to enjoy a walk to the delights of Riddlesdown or up Foxley Lane to the Webb estate to see the roses in season.

up along the tram routes at Norbury, Purley and Addiscombe.

Following the 1902 Education Act, the School Board was replaced by the Corporation's Education Committee and the Borough (later Selhurst Grammar) Schools were established in 1904. Central Schools (later John Ruskin, Lady Edridge and Heath Clark) soon followed, and special schools for mentally and physically handicapped children also opened from 1911. Between the wars new schools were built in areas of population growth and some of the old, inadequate schools were provided with new buildings. Some under-resourced Anglican schools were closed.

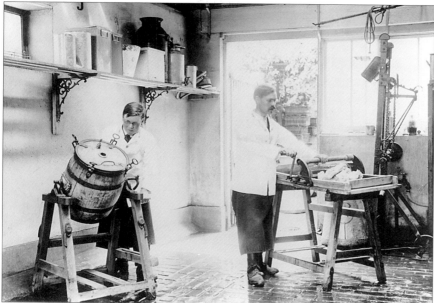

105 *Farming remained very labour-intensive until the 20th century, as illustrated by this photograph of harvesting at Waddon Court Farm in 1907. It was quite usual for the children to assist with the harvest and they often played truant from school for the purpose.*

106 *This undated photograph shows butter-making in Croydon around the beginning of the 20th century.*

107 Welford's Surrey Dairies was based in Croydon and had several shops around the town, including this one at no. 193 Brighton Road. Their deliveries in the area were by handcart. Virtually all traders would deliver goods to the home until after the Second World War, and many used horse-drawn vehicles.

A very interesting residential development had started at Purley just beyond the then borough boundary. William Webb, a Croydon estate agent, purchased 260 acres of downland in 1888 and, in order to pursue his ideal of an estate with a rural character, he immediately cleared the land of all fences and started planting trees at least 12 years old. Before any house was started he planned the whole estate, with curving roads, bordered by trees, grass or flower beds and established a nursery where he propagated trees and shrubs. Services such as gas, water, drainage and electricity were buried underground and the roads were fully made up before building started in 1898.

A lower cost limit was set for the houses, and attention was paid to the design of the rear and sides as much as to the front of each. There were

108 Brickwood House and estate was privately occupied at the beginning of the 20th century. The last resident was Thomas Reid. Although only just across the road from East Croydon station, cattle still grazed there when this photograph was taken in 1908. The owners had offered part of the Cherry Orchard Road frontage for sale as early as 1867 but there seem not to have been any buyers.

no wooden fences, only wire fences and hedges. A large 'village' green was laid out with pond, geese, whipping post, stocks and a smithy. The *Lord Roberts*, a temperance inn, was named after one of Webb's heroes. The estate was completed in 1925 and is now a Conservation Area. William Webb wrote a book, *Garden First in Land Development*, and his estate pre-dated the Garden City idea.

Joe Rosenthal, a cameraman who filmed in the South African War, settled in Croydon High Street in 1906 and formed the Rosie Film Company,

making films in his back garden as well as one of the first true documentaries of *Life On A North Sea Trawler*. Another pioneer called Hassan also made films at premises in the High Street. In 1904 the Clarendon Film Company was formed at Limes Road, and another company, Cricks and Martin, was set up soon afterwards. There was still plenty of open country and hilly places around as well as disused gravel pits, ideal for location shots. Many films were made locally until the First World War, but the companies had gone by 1920.

109 *In 1907 the whole estate of 16 acres was offered for sale but it was not until 1908 that 27 separate building plots fronting Cherry Orchard and Addiscombe Roads were actually sold.*

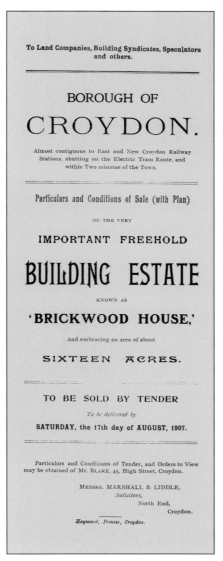

To Land Companies, Building Syndicates, Speculators and others.

BOROUGH OF

CROYDON.

Almost contiguous to East and New Croydon Railway Stations, abutting on the Electric Tram Route, and within Two minutes of the Town.

Particulars and Conditions of Sale (with Plan)

OF THE VERY

IMPORTANT FREEHOLD

BUILDING ESTATE

KNOWN AS

'BRICKWOOD HOUSE,'

And embracing an area of about

SIXTEEN ACRES.

TO BE SOLD BY TENDER

To be delivered by

SATURDAY, the 17th day of AUGUST, 1907.

Particulars and Conditions of Tender, and Orders to View may be obtained of Mr. BLAKE, 45, High Street, Croydon.

MESSRS. MARSHALL & LIDDLE,
Solicitors,
North End,
Croydon.

Hayward, Printer, Croydon.

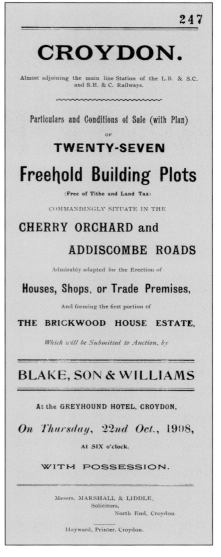

247

CROYDON.

Almost adjoining the main line Station of the L.B. & S.C. and S.E. & C. Railways.

Particulars and Conditions of Sale (with Plan)

OF

TWENTY-SEVEN

Freehold Building Plots

(Free of Tithe and Land Tax)

COMMANDINGLY SITUATE IN THE

CHERRY ORCHARD and

ADDISCOMBE ROADS

Admirably adapted for the Erection of

Houses, Shops, or Trade Premises,

And forming the first portion of

THE BRICKWOOD HOUSE ESTATE,

Which will be Submitted to Auction, by

BLAKE, SON & WILLIAMS

At the GREYHOUND HOTEL, CROYDON,

On *Thursday, 22nd Oct., 1908,*

At SIX o'clock.

WITH POSSESSION.

Messrs. MARSHALL & LIDDLE,
Solicitors,
North End, Croydon.

Hayward, Printer, Croydon.

110 *(above left)   This view of Addiscombe Road shows a sale board for part of the Brickwood Estate, and a few houses in Colson Road that were built in 1910. A roller-skating rink was built on the corner site in about 1910 and this had become Creed's factory by 1916.*

111 *(left)   The Public Halls in George Street were opened in 1860 and leased by the Croydon Literary and Scientific Institution until it was wound up in 1929. The halls were then taken over by Croydon Council and demolished around 1958 as part of the town centre redevelopment programme.*

112 *(above)   The Stanley Halls in South Norwood Hill were designed and provided by William Ford Stanley, who lived at Cumberlow Lodge, a house he had built on the former Pascall's brickfield. Stanley was a creative man and invented numerous machines and drawing instruments. He established the Stanley Technical Trade School. The somewhat strange architecture of the halls led Sir Nikolaus Pevsner to describe the buildings as 'one of the most eccentric efforts anywhere at a do-it-yourself free style'. The building is Grade II listed, as is the Stanley Memorial Clocktower at the top of Station Road. Stanley was South Norwood's, and one of Croydon's, greatest benefactors and died in 1909.*

Another local industry was lavender and herb growing. It was carried on in the Mitcham area for centuries but reached a peak in the mid-19th century having spread out to Wallington, Carshalton, Croydon and Norwood. Housing development gradually covered the fields and it seems to have ceased locally by the Second World War. The Distillery in Mitcham Road, Croydon continued to work until 1949.

William Gillett established a clock-making business in 1844 and a few years later he was joined by Charles Bland and they started making turret clocks. In 1877 Arthur Johnston became a partner and by the early 20th century the firm had become world-famous as Gillett and Johnston. The works were in Whitehorse Road but closed in the mid-1950s, though the company still exists in a small way, dealing in clocks but not bells.

113 (left) *The Station Picture Hall in Station Road, West Croydon was the first cinema in the town. It opened in a converted shop in May 1908, offering half-an-hour of living pictures for a penny, and seating 120 people in somewhat cramped conditions. It was later the West Croydon Picture Hall, and later still the King's Picture Hall. It closed around 1917.*

114 (below) *The magnificent Davis' Theatre was the fourth largest cinema in the country, with 3,678 seats. It opened in December 1928 and in 1944 was hit by a German bomb which did not explode, fortunately, for there were 2,000 patrons in the building at the time. Nevertheless, six people were killed and 25 injured. Apart from films, concerts, opera and ballet were frequently on offer, and in 1956 the Bolshoi Ballet made its only appearance in England there, apart from Covent Garden. The queue for tickets stretched from the theatre to East Croydon station. The Davis closed in 1959 and was demolished, to be replaced by an office block, Davis House.*

115 (right) *This plan shows the position of all 41 cinemas that have existed in the borough at one time or another. The original names are given but a number later changed names several times.*

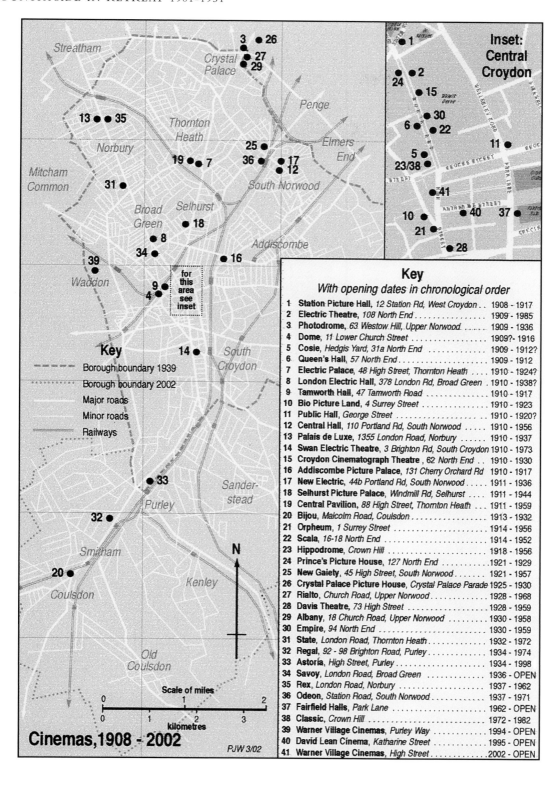

Key
With opening dates in chronological order

1 **Station Picture Hall**, *12 Station Rd, West Croydon* . . 1908 - 1917
2 **Electric Theatre**, *108 North End* . . . . 1909 - 1985
3 **Photodrome**, *63 Westow Hill, Upper Norwood* . . . . . . 1909 - 1936
4 **Dome**, *11 Lower Church Street* . . . . 1909?- 1916
5 **Cosie**, *Hedgis Yard, 31a North End* . . . . 1909 - 1912?
6 **Queen's Hall**, *57 North End* . . . . 1909 - 1912
7 **Electric Palace**, *48 High Street, Thornton Heath* . . . 1910 - 1924?
8 **London Electric Hall**, *378 London Rd, Broad Green* . . 1910 - 1938?
9 **Tamworth Hall**, *47 Tamworth Road* . . . . 1910 - 1917
10 **Bio Picture Land**, *4 Surrey Street* . . . . 1910 - 1923
11 **Public Hall**, *George Street* . . . . 1910 - 1920?
12 **Central Hall**, *110 Portland Rd, South Norwood* . . . . . 1910 - 1956
13 **Palais de Luxe**, *1355 London Road, Norbury* . . . . . . 1910 - 1937
14 **Swan Electric Theatre**, *3 Brighton Rd, South Croydon* 1910 - 1973
15 **Croydon Cinematograph Theatre** , *62 North End* . . 1910 - 1930
16 **Addiscombe Picture Palace**, *131 Cherry Orchard Rd* 1910 - 1917
17 **New Electric**, *44b Portland Rd, South Norwood* . . . . . 1911 - 1936
18 **Selhurst Picture Palace**, *Windmill Rd, Selhurst* . . . . 1911 - 1944
19 **Central Pavilion**, *88 High Street, Thornton Heath* . . . 1911 - 1959
20 **Bijou**, *Malcolm Road, Coulsdon* . . . . 1913 - 1932
21 **Orpheum**, *1 Surrey Street* . . . . 1914 - 1956
22 **Scala**, *16-18 North End* . . . . 1914 - 1952
23 **Hippodrome**, *Crown Hill* . . . . 1918 - 1956
24 **Prince's Picture House**, *127 North End* . . . . .1921 - 1929
25 **New Gaiety**, *45 High Street, South Norwood* . . . . . . 1921 - 1957
26 **Crystal Palace Picture House**, *Crystal Palace Parade* 1925 - 1930
27 **Rialto**, *Church Road, Upper Norwood* . . . . 1928 - 1968
28 **Davis Theatre**, *73 High Street* . . . . 1928 - 1959
29 **Albany**, *18 Church Road, Upper Norwood* . . . . 1930 - 1958
30 **Empire**, *94 North End* . . . . 1930 - 1959
31 **State**, *London Road, Thornton Heath* . . . . 1932 - 1972
32 **Regal**, *92 - 98 Brighton Road, Purley* . . . . 1934 - 1974
33 **Astoria**, *High Street, Purley* . . . . 1934 - 1998
34 **Savoy**, *London Road, Broad Green* . . . . 1936 - OPEN
35 **Rex**, *London Road, Norbury* . . . . 1937 - 1962
36 **Odeon**, *Station Road, South Norwood* . . . . 1937 - 1971
37 **Fairfield Halls**, *Park Lane* . . . . 1962 - OPEN
38 **Classic**, *Crown Hill* . . . . 1972 - 1982
39 **Warner Village Cinemas**, *Purley Way* . . . . 1994 - OPEN
40 **David Lean Cinema**, *Katharine Street* . . . . 1995 - OPEN
41 **Warner Village Cinemas**, *High Street* . . . . 2002 - OPEN

Cinemas, 1908 - 2002

PJW 3/02

116 *The Holy Innocents' Church in Selhurst Road, South Norwood was just one of many that had their own sports teams. Here the football team are seen with their cup as champions of the Thornton Heath & District League for the 1919-20 season.*

First World War

In *Croydon and The Great War*, the initial effect of the outbreak of war on 4 August 1914 is described as follows:

> Anyone walking through Croydon streets on the day after War had been declared, would hear that in the night a military train had passed along the London, Brighton and South Coast Railway, and had dropped guards, who were men drawn from the City of London Volunteers, at bridges, signal boxes and other vulnerable points; there were sentries already in position at water reservoirs, gas and electricity works and similar places ... Grave-faced knots of people discussed the situation at every corner, and in every shop, office and restaurant ... moving quietly through the streets are Volunteers of the Croydon National Reserve selecting and commandeering horses and vehicles from firms who are considered able to spare them ... Next day we learn that train services have been severely restricted, all cheap tickets being withdrawn ... Yet a few hours, and the walls of

117 *As Croydon expanded so local district centres grew up. Purley and Norbury had very few shops in 1900 but the arrival of the electric trams stimulated housing development and shopping parades soon followed. Addiscombe was developing its own small centre near the tram terminus by 1907 and this photograph dates from around 1910. The railway bridge carrying the Woodside and South Croydon Railway is in the background and would soon be surrounded by shops. After the railway line closed the bridge was demolished and there is now a street-level crossing for Tramlink on the site.*

118 *South Norwood developed after the London and Croydon Railway opened in 1839. A few shops appeared from the 1840s in Portland Road and in the High Street near the station from the 1860s. It was a flourishing local centre by the late 1890s and this postcard view of the High Street, looking north-east, dates from about 1910. South Norwood Hill is on the left, and Portland Road opposite to the right. Most of the local shopping centres such as this have declined in importance since the 1950s with the growth of private car use and the development of supermarkets.*

119 *Thornton Heath High Street developed as a local shopping centre from the 1860s. On the right is the Central Cinema which opened in 1911 and was renamed the Pavilion in 1921. It became the Pullman in 1956 and closed in 1959. Thornton Heath Clock Tower is in the distance to the right of the tram.*

120 *In 1906 Croydon Corporation built an estate of 'workman's dwellings' to the east of Spring Lane. This view shows Corporation Road (now Longhurst Road) with the general shop (right) on the corner of Spring Lane. The corporation produced an illustrated leaflet describing the amenities of the houses, from the 'thin solid patent fireproof partitions' which divided the bedrooms 'thus saving valuable space' to the flat concrete roof over the scullery and outside WC. 'The scullery has a food cupboard, portable copper, and a strong brown glazed sink on glazed brick bearers'. The weekly rent was 6s. 6d.*

121 *A workman at Gillett and Johnston's Bell Foundry pours molten metal into a mould around 1920. In those days factory work could be quite hazardous. Health and safety requirements were not nearly as rigorous as today.*

122 *Workmen at John Jakson's Peppermint Distillery in Mitcham Road around 1930. The distillery closed in 1949.*

123 *William Bennett's sandpits and yard at Shirley was started in 1777. The company expanded into coach operation for some years, but continued their rural crafts until closure in the 1980s.*

the town were plastered with the words, TO THE RECRUITING OFFICE, with huge arrows pointing the way … Khaki became familiar in our streets.

Thousands of local people soon volunteered for service. Many Croydonians went to war and, sadly, over 2,500 never returned.

There were numerous local warnings of zeppelin attacks, but very few serious incidents. However, on 13 October 1915, 18 bombs were dropped on the town, killing 11 people, injuring 17, and damaging 800 buildings.

124 (above left) *This photograph shows the mobilisation of the Croydon Territorials on 5 August 1914. The original barracks building in the background was built in 1794, and was one of the first purpose-built barracks in the country. Initially, cavalry were stationed there, but in 1803 the Royal Waggon Train moved in. In the mid-19th century, before Caterham Barracks was built, the Guards Depot was housed here. The original building was demolished in the 1960s but the barracks remain in use by Territorial Army units.*

125 (above right) *During the First World War six council schools in Croydon were converted into War Hospitals, with 1,000 beds. Children from the closed schools were redistributed to others. This photograph was taken at the Crescent War Hospital (later Selhurst Grammar School).*

Aviation

In 1915 an airfield was opened at Beddington as part of the Air Defence of London. Then, in 1918, National Aircraft Factory Number 1 was built at Waddon, together with a flying ground for testing aircraft built there. This large factory employing over 2,100 people ceased work only a few months later when the war ended in November 1918. Some 1,500 workers were dismissed and marched on Croydon Town Hall in protest. The factory was converted to a salvage depot run by the Aircraft Disposal Company. Beddington and Waddon airfields were combined to form Croydon Aerodrome, which became the customs airport for London in 1920. Trust Houses Ltd wanted to replace the canteen with a hotel but had some difficulty in obtaining a licence as the Chairman of the Bench wondered 'if it was suggested that passengers might arrive in such a condition that a little alcohol might be required'. The licence was granted and Croydon was the first aerodrome in England to offer hotel meals and accommodation for travellers.

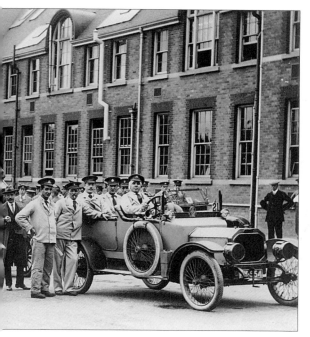

126 *Allotments were provided by the council before 1906. They became more popular during the First World War, as this postcard view demonstrates. In 1918 it was claimed that the town had one third of the total acreage in the county of Surrey. There are still many allotments in various parts of the town, but their popularity has diminished since the Second World War, and some have been used for building purposes.*

127 *After the end of the First World War war memorials were put up by numerous schools, factories and other organisations. The town's principal war memorial is outside the Town Hall in Katharine Street. This photograph shows the dedication ceremony of the Croydon Corporation Tramways war memorial at Purley Tram Depot.*

128 The new Croydon Airport terminal buildings on Purley Way opened in 1928. Here one of the famous Handley Page HP 42s flies over the airport in the early 1930s, with Purley Way Playing Fields and the South Croydon valley beyond.

As air travel expanded the primitive facilities proved inadequate, and in 1928 a completely new terminal, purpose-built hotel and airfield opened adjacent to Purley Way. This road had opened in 1925 as a by-pass for Croydon. The airport became the scene for many of the great inaugural flights in aviation and the name of Croydon became known throughout the world as a result. When the Second World War broke out civil flying ceased and the airport played its part in the Battle of Britain. Civil flying resumed in 1946 until the airport closed in 1959. It was not large enough for the latest passenger planes being developed and Gatwick took its place, as it had taken the place of Woodside in horse racing 70 years earlier.

Between the Wars

By the time of the 1921 census Croydon's population was 191,375 and was set to increase by a further 42,000 over the next ten years. Until the 20th century it was common for most people to rent rather than own property. Even by 1914 only about ten per cent of all dwellings were owner-occupied but the big change came between the wars. By 1939 the proportion of owner-occupied dwellings had increased to 31 per cent. In the inter-war years office workers, teachers, shopkeepers and better paid industrial workers in regular employment joined the ranks of property owners, although many others were excluded. By 1939 only about eighteen per cent of working-class families were owner-occupiers, and for some of them the new local authority housing of the 1920s was an acceptable alternative, but many still aspired to home ownership and could not afford it. Small-holdings were provided, particularly for ex-servicemen, by County Councils at Selsdon for example, but these provided only a spartan existence. In the absence of rigorous planning controls, those aspiring to owner-occupation could often obtain a cheap plot of land and build their own shack, or place on it a ready-made wooden building such as an old tram, bus or railway carriage. As a result, not all housing estate developments proceeded smoothly, and the environmental benefits enjoyed by the residents of the Webb estate at Purley were certainly not repeated everywhere. Dr Cox researched Ham Farm in Shirley in the 1960s and interviewed some of the original residents. He found a very different situation.

Ham Farm formed part of a much larger estate called Monks Orchard. The whole estate was put up for sale in 46 lots in 1920 but much remained unsold. Most of the land was bought by Percy Harvey Estates of Margate, who produced a brochure offering 'residential sites; and park, meadow and arable, exceptionally attractive for fruit growing, poultry farming, market gardening and small holdings'. No attempt was made to construct or plan additional roads and all the lots fronted existing farm tracks. Some of the plots were 1,000 feet deep, and at first only one house could be erected on each, although this restriction was soon lifted. The first premises were poultry farms, nurseries, a market garden and a fruit farm. Some properties were built without the necessary Fitness of Habitation Certificate required under the 1875 Public Health Act and 1877 Model Bye-laws.

There were no services on the estate and some householders had to walk up to half a mile along the farm tracks to get their water, whilst others, on the north side, fetched it in cans from a house in Long Lane. The cess-pits were cleared only intermittently by Croydon Council, there was no electricity, and people had to walk up to 1½ miles to Elmers End to fetch paraffin for their oil lamps. The roads were very bad; in 1926 a surveyor lost his chain in the mud of Orchard Avenue, and in bad weather people had to cling to the chestnut palings to make progress along the road. No motor

vehicles could gain access for much of the time. It was not until 1924 that bus services started along Wickham Road and Long Lane.

This type of problem nationally led to greater planning control, and by the 1930s public utility services were provided. The roads were being adopted and properly surfaced but the layout is still based on the old farm tracks, with numerous culs-de-sac leading off culs-de-sac and inaccessible areas of land. The fate of Ham Farm House was equally bizarre. In 1925 it was sold to the wife of Harry Cameron, the stage illusionist known as the Great Carmo. The house became known as Carmo Manor and the barns and outhouses were used to house his menagerie during the winter. The residents of an area barely two miles from the centre of Surrey's largest town were not only living under very difficult conditions, being almost cut off at times, but their sleep was likely to be disturbed by the roaring of lions! Carmo Manor was later vacated

129   *This postcard view of The Glade, Ham Farm shows the winding nature of the farm track which was used as one of the main roads on the estate. It was taken around 1923 from approximately where Greenview Avenue was later built on the right. The bungalow in the left distance is now nos. 149 and 149A The Glade. Note the temporary nature of the wooden house in the centre. The postcard has the following message on the back: 'My land runs right through the wood seen in the distance. Saw rabbits and a pheasant in my part of the wood on Saturday last – Percy'.*

130 *Howden Road, off South Norwood Hill, was first laid out in the 1880s when houses were built on the left. For nearly forty years the residents could enjoy the view over the fields on the right, with Norwood Lake and Sports Club at the bottom of the road.*

131 *The residents also had this rural view at the back, with fields, woods and the Crystal Palace in the distance.*

132 *The rural surroundings of Howden Road lasted until the 1920s. Then the houses on the right were built between about 1925 and 1927. As with so many roads, parked cars now disfigure its appearance.*

133   *Canham Road, off Whitehorse Lane, South Norwood illustrates several periods of gradual development. The large Victorian house at the top of the hill is Kilravock, built in about 1864 by Major Ross, when it stood in grounds of seven acres. The road named after him was formerly the drive to the house from South Norwood Hill. The house has been used as flats for years, and following a fire has recently been renovated. It forms a very conspicuous landmark for miles around.*

The four houses on the immediate left were built in the early 1890s. One still had the covered way from the pavement to the front door when this photograph was taken in about 1930. The other houses were all built between about 1927 and 1934. The electricity sub-station on the right is one of many built by the Croydon Corporation Electricity Department to resemble the domestic architecture of the period.

134   *By the 1920s housing development began to spread inexorably on to the downs south of Croydon, although the view from Croham Hurst towards Sanderstead in about 1922 was still very rural.*

135   This old cottage, no.8 Pump Pail, was a relic of many similar buildings in the Old Town area. Most had gone by 1934 when this picture was taken and Croydon Corporation was replacing such structures with new council houses. The Gillam family seen here ran 'Bunny's' stall in Surrey Street.

and used for lead-foil smelting, until this was banned as a nuisance and the house was demolished.

Most of the new building between the wars was taking place in the remaining open land to the north of the town, and in the Waddon, Croham and Shirley areas made more accessible by new motor bus services. Some of the new developments consisted of several roads of more or less identical houses, such as the Elm Park, Norhyrst and Falkland Park estates in South Norwood which were built in the late 1920s and early 1930s. In the case of the former the houses were terraced and a tennis club with several courts was provided behind Elm Park Road. The Norhyrst estate was a mixture of terraced and slightly larger semi-detached houses, and residents had the facilities of Norwood Club in Avenue Road nearby. Falkland Park consisted of terraced houses, and residents could enjoy nearby Grange Wood with its bowling greens and tennis courts. The original Falkland Park mansion and a small part of the once extensive wooded grounds are now Spurgeon's College, a training establishment for Baptist ministers.

Selsdon Garden Village estate was started by Richard Costain and Sons in 1925. It was over a mile from the nearest development and the first houses were in Byron, Farley and Queenhill roads. Residents originally had to walk to South Croydon for shops and trains but after a while Costain's put on a bus service until the East Surrey Traction Company introduced a regular service in 1926. The name of the estate was soon changed to Croham Heights which sounded rather better.

Many of the people who first moved into estates such as these were newly married couples. Their children grew up, played and went to school together. Few of the women had jobs; there was quite enough to do at home in the days before the advent of modern labour-saving devices. There were few cars and most people walked to the local shops or used buses so they got to know many of their neighbours. A sense of community developed that lasted beyond the Second World War but which the greater mobility made possible by the spread of motoring has increasingly eroded.

With the 1925 opening of Purley Way as a by-pass for the town, a number of factories were built on the adjacent land. By the late 1930s these were occupied by companies such as Trojan Motors, Croydon Foundry, Standard Steel, Aeronautical & General Industries, Metal Propellors, Powers Accounting Machines, Southern Foundries, Redwings, Philips and Waterman's Dyeing and Cleaning Works. Several of these companies had aviation interests and were no doubt attracted to the area by the nearby airport. Small pockets of industry and isolated factories remained in many other parts of the town.

Leisure activities were increasingly well catered for. Golf had become popular early in the century, the first local course being Beckenham, partly on the site of the former Croydon Racecourse. The North Surrey Golf Course at Norbury opened in

136 *This aerial view of New Addington dates from about 1936. The original Lodge Lane can be seen wending its way south into the countryside.*

137 *This mid-1930s view of Church Street shows how much busier it used to be than it is in the early 21st century. The road was at that time still surfaced with tarred wooden blocks, a fairly common material at the time.*

138 Croydon's three large department stores attracted shoppers from as far away as the south coast. Kennard's, on the left, and Allder's, on the right, were a very familiar feature of the town. Allder's remains a well-known name but Kennard's has been replaced by Debenham's and the Drummond Centre.

about 1898, and others such as Croham Hurst, Addington, Shirley Park and Purley Downs which soon followed, have ensured the survival of attractive green areas that might otherwise have been built upon. Croydon Corporation was active in providing new parks and recreation grounds: Grange Wood was acquired in 1900 and, after a lengthy public campaign, Croham Hurst was purchased in 1901, thus frustrating the Whitgift Foundation's intention to build on it. By 1939 there were 46 sites totalling 1,197 acres in council ownership. Some of these were not as yet open to the public, and there were more in the Coulsdon and Purley area.

Other sports such as cricket and football were played by numerous local teams, and some of the banks and other business houses had their own sports and social clubs. Professional football came to Croydon when Crystal Palace Football Club moved to the former Croydon Common ground at Selhurst just after the First World War. The present ground at Selhurst Park became the new home in 1924 and the club is regarded as Croydon's team.

The cinema had become increasingly popular after the First World War and new 'super cinemas' were being built. In 1928 the Davis' Theatre was opened in the High Street. The auditorium had the

second largest seating capacity in the country – 3,725. With a fully-equipped stage, the theatre was the venue for opera, ballet, concerts, etc., as well as films. It was named after the family who owned it. In 1946 the Royal Philharmonic Orchestra gave its first performance there, under the baton of Sir Thomas Beecham. Other cinemas of more modest proportions soon appeared elsewhere in the town. There was a lot of controversy locally over Sunday opening of cinemas. Despite a petition in 1927 containing 24,000 signatures in favour, the council rejected Sunday opening by 34 votes to eleven. However, a town poll in 1932 attracted a massive turnout of over half the electorate. A crowd of 8,000 people gathered outside the Town Hall to hear the result declared – 34,617 voted for Sunday opening, and 24,386 voted against. The Suffragan Bishop of Croydon had supported the proposal, hoping that the right kind of film would help people 'to be more healthy minded – to be in fact mentally and morally better men and women'. The whole affair is an indication of the much greater interest taken by people in local matters 70 years ago than today.

There were numerous local societies covering a variety of interests. In 1914 Alan Kirby had formed the Croydon Sacred Harmonic Society, which was reorganised as the Croydon Philharmonic Society in 1919. It became famous outside Croydon for its performances of the works of Elgar, and continues its concerts in the 21st century. Amateur dramatics were popular, and Croydon Stagers and the Croydon Operatic and Dramatic Association (CODA) continue to entertain local audiences with their productions.

The motor vehicle became increasingly reliable after the First World War. In 1921 the East Surrey Traction Company started running bus routes from Croydon to Sevenoaks, Edenbridge and Redhill. Other routes to Guildford, Hartfield and Uckfield soon followed, and enabled crowds to ride out into the nearby countryside. In 1923 the nation's railways were merged into four large companies. Locally the London, Brighton and South Coast, and South Eastern and Chatham railways became part of the Southern Railway. Electrification spread rapidly during the 1930s, adding to the attractiveness of areas to the south of the town for residential development.

In 1930 the duties of the Board of Guardians passed to Croydon Corporation, whose responsibilities were then at their widest. In 1933 the local tramways were absorbed into the newly formed London Passenger Transport Board, which soon started the process of converting tram routes to trolleybus operation. The routes to Sutton, Crystal Palace and Mitcham were converted by 1937 but further conversion of local routes was halted by the war. Addington parish had been added to Croydon in 1928, and in 1935 work started on a housing estate high on the North Downs. The development, known as New Addington, was commenced by Henry Boot and Company on land purchased by the Corporation.

In 1936 the Crystal Palace was destroyed by fire. It had been a popular venue for local people during its 80 years on the Norwood heights. A landmark for miles around, it was greatly missed, and its loss led to general decline in the fortunes of the Upper Norwood area. In 1937 a typhoid epidemic resulted in 344 cases and 43 deaths. It was indirectly caused by a total lack of communication between the Medical Officer of Health and the Borough Engineer. The council came under attack nationally for its dilatoriness in making known the facts and in suggesting preventative action by householders. It stated that there was no cause for alarm (which there was), that it was doing everything it could to arrest the spread of the epidemic (which it wasn't), and that watercress might be the cause (which was untrue and brought the wrath of the entire Watercress Growers' Section of the National Union of Farmers down on the heads of the councillors).

Second World War

The possibility of war became apparent in the mid-1930s and Croydon Corporation established an Air Raid Precautions Committee in 1935. War was declared on 3 September 1939 and large numbers of local children were immediately evacuated, mainly to Brighton and Hove. The first bombs to fall near London exploded on farmland at Addington on 17/18 June 1940. Croydon experienced its first raid on 15 August 1940 when a number of bombs dropped on and around Croydon Airport. In total 62 people were killed, and 37 were seriously and 137 less seriously injured. With Kenley and Biggin Hill airfields nearby it was inevitable that Croydon would be subject to attack, and for some weeks the Battle of Britain raged overhead. The sound of machine-gun and anti-aircraft fire filled the air, and the sky was criss-crossed with vapour trails and puffs of smoke, the aircraft gleaming as silver specks in the clear blue skies. The Blitz followed and the area suffered many raids, although not to the extent of London's East End nor some provincial cities. Air raids continued at intervals through to May 1941, by which time 362 Croydon people had been killed and 672 sent to hospital. Over 1,000 houses had been destroyed. These figures exclude the Coulsdon and Purley area.

K.M. King, schoolmaster at Selhurst Grammar School for Boys, kept a detailed diary for some fifty

139   The Second World War saw great efforts to collect salvage, and here books are being collected to aid the war effort. Salvage Shops were set up in many parts of the town as collection centres.

years. This extract gives a vivid impression of the air raid on the night of 16/17 April 1941:

> The barrage guns were thundering on all sides, and searchlights turned the dark into a bright, white twilight … Then soon after ten o'clock, we heard a clatter which we thought was that of slates falling from the roof … the noise had been that of the falling of incendiary bombs, a dozen of them, by this time blazing furiously … fire parties and wardens of The Crescent and the immediate district were all rallying and in the midst of the awful spectacle their appearance was really comic; mostly women, they came running along, blowing whistles to give the alarm, and most of them carrying dust-bin lids for protection … We stayed for nearly an hour watching a display of the fire-works of war that would be described as gorgeous if it were not so sinister. Searchlights still probed the pale night sky, and against their light shells burst like rockets; in three directions the sky was reddened with the glare of fires, smudged with columns of smoke; red tracer bullets described graceful arcs; and two groups of pale yellow flares drifted slowly down, shedding a brilliant light. It was a beautiful rather than a terrifying spectacle. There was, of course, a continuous accompaniment of sound, mainly the bursting of shells and the ringing of ambulance and fire-engine bells. Then as we

stood watching and listening, there was a sudden reddish glow, a loud explosion, and, while we still felt the movement of rushing air, the sudden tinkling of shattered glass … This is the nearest we have been to falling bombs, and somehow I am not in the least frightened but simply exhilarated and excited – I should have been sorry to miss it.

After May 1941 air raids were light and sporadic. Many of the evacuated children returned home. In mid-June 1944 the flying bombs (known as V1s or 'doodlebugs') began to rain on the town and rapid plans had to be made to re-evacuate children whose parents wished them to go. The town suffered very

140 (facing page, top)   The town was quite badly bombed during the Second World War, but most damage was inflicted by the V1 Flying Bombs, or 'Doodle Bugs', in 1944. This photograph is typical of so many scenes of devastation in the Croydon area, and shows the effects of a V1 which fell in Moffatt Road, Thornton Heath on the night of 4/5 July 1944. The Salvation Army was one of several organisations that gave assistance at such incidents by providing refreshments for rescue workers and people rendered homeless.

141 (facing page, bottom)   The Home Guard consisted of men in reserved occupations or who were too old or unfit for regular service. This shows the last march-past in Katharine Street of the local Home Guard when it was stood down on 26 November 1944. Sir Malcolm Fraser, Lord Lieutenant of Surrey, took the salute from outside the Town Hall.

badly, with 141 landing in the borough and a further 54 in the Coulsdon and Purley area. Several V2 rockets also fell on the town. To help with repairs to property, 1,500 building workers were drafted into the town from various parts of the country.

During the war years a large number of service men and women were stationed in the area. Theatres, cinemas, dance halls and public houses were well patronised. There were numerous big parades in support of various national savings and fund-raising events. As an example, Salute the Soldier Week in 1944 saw a two-mile-long procession through the town, including the bands of the Welsh Guards, Royal Air Force, the East Yorkshire Regiment and Metropolitan Police, while the band of the Royal Marines, Chatham entertained the crowds in Katharine Street. The aim of the week was to raise sufficient savings in the town to equip a tank regiment.

142   This 1940s view of Addington Church shows the rural and peaceful atmosphere of the village which persisted until the 1960s. Lodge Lane winds its way up the hill towards New Addington, then still a relatively small settlement.

The Post-War Years

The town celebrated the end of the war with parties, bonfires and dancing in the streets. But there were many problems during the next few years. A serious housing shortage and a backlog of repairs and maintenance to most property, with a continuation of rationing until the early 1950s, meant this was a period of austerity.

Croydon Council soon started a major building programme and prefabricated houses were erected on numerous vacant sites. But many parts of the town presented a run-down and generally dowdy appearance. The 1947 winter brought six weeks of snow and ice, severe fuel shortages, and 12,000 local people laid off work! Offices and shops had heating for only a few hours each day, and people had to work in coats and gloves. In 1948 the foundation stone of the new Croydon 'B' power station was laid, and the Corporation's electricity undertaking was nationalised. The Croydon Gas Company was absorbed into the nationalised gas industry, and the local hospitals passed from council control to the new National Health Service.

Tremendous social changes had taken place during the previous half century. The position of women in particular had altered as a result of the two world wars. They were now on a much more equal footing with men. Few people could afford the domestic staff which had been almost a necessity for the middle classes at the beginning of the century. No longer was there a tacit acceptance of authority. If one had feared God and Croydon Corporation in that order in 1900, the latter was likely to be a greater cause for concern by 1950.

The town's last trams ran on Saturday 7 April 1951, to be replaced by motor buses. The large crowds that gathered to bid farewell could not have imagined that their modern equivalent would return to the local streets within fifty years.

VIII

Suburban Centre to Edge City 1951-2001

IN 1951 the population of Croydon was 249,570. Food rationing was still in force and would not be completely ended until 1954. The Festival of Britain in 1951 was intended to celebrate the centenary of the Great Exhibition of 1851 and to provide a lift to a country still suffering the effects of war. It was described as 'A Tonic To The Nation'. The celebrations in Croydon were fairly low-key, the main contribution being the Corporation's Ashburton Memorial Homes at Addiscombe.

In 1952 the sudden and unexpected death of King George VI shocked the country. The Coronation of Queen Elizabeth II in 1953 signalled a new era. Television became increasingly widespread, affecting the size of audiences in cinemas and theatres which were closing fast. The Scala in North End closed in March 1952 and the Empire Theatre was converted to the Eros Cinema in 1953. Other cinemas also closed, but the biggest shocks to the town came in 1959 when the splendid Victorian Grand Theatre and the huge Davis' Theatre closed.

Croydon's town centre at this time remained modest in scale in relation to the population. In 1955 the council approved a redevelopment scheme and in 1956 the Croydon Corporation Act was passed. It gave the local authority the power to buy land compulsorily without having to justify itself to the Ministry of Housing and Local Government. Having acquired two acres of land in multiple ownership and added two acres of its own (including the site of the Public Halls), the council leased the part not required for road widening to private developers for shop and office building. The first

office block, Norfolk House, proved so successful in attracting tenants that others, Suffolk House and Essex House, soon followed. The area became known locally as Little East Anglia. Developers soon saw the potential of other sites in central Croydon and site values and rents rose.

Meanwhile the council was planning a new concert hall and theatre at Fairfield, to be partly funded from the old Public Halls site in George Street and the sale of the Civic Hall at Crown Hill and North End. A surprise objection to the Fairfield Halls led to a town poll, the first such for 27 years, but there was a very small turnout compared with the Sunday opening of cinemas campaign of the 1930s, and the vote was in favour of the project, so the Halls were built. They were formally opened by Queen Elizabeth the Queen Mother in November 1962. The complex consists of a large concert hall, the Ashcroft Theatre and the Arnhem Gallery, with smaller meeting rooms, bars and catering facilities. The concert hall has attracted many famous artists and is justly famed for the excellent acoustics.

The London County Council and the Ministry of Housing and Local Government were at the time taking measures to combat congestion in central London, and to encourage decentralisation of offices. Croydon Corporation earmarked an area of about forty-five acres for offices in the north-east part of the town centre occupied mainly by large Victorian houses and two schools. By 1969 over 3½ million square feet of office space was complete and 1½ million square feet was under construction. There were already 45 large office

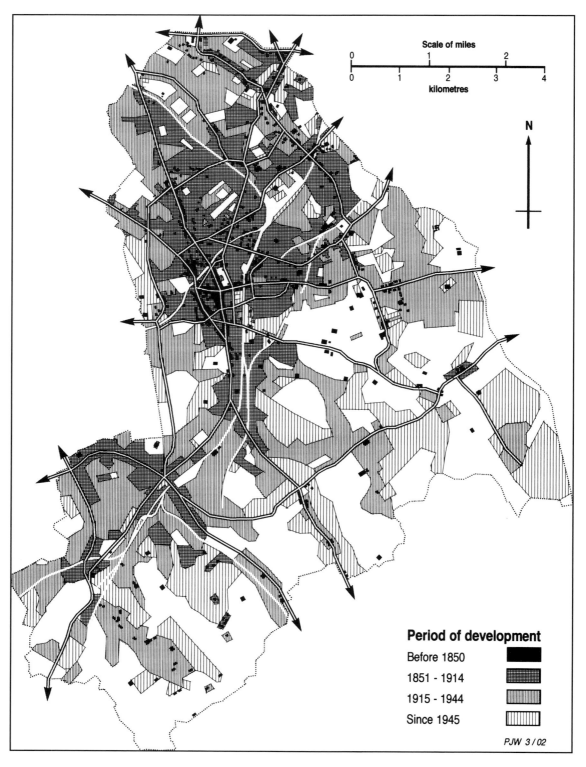

Scale of miles

0   1   2

0   1   2   3   4
kilometres

N

Period of development

Before 1850

1851 - 1914

1915 - 1944

Since 1945

PJW 3 / 02

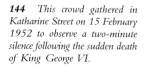

144 *This crowd gathered in Katharine Street on 15 February 1952 to observe a two-minute silence following the sudden death of King George VI.*

blocks, half of which were over ten storeys high. They became a striking, if sometimes overpowering, feature of the landscape, but certainly made the town centre a landmark for miles around.

Undoubtedly the leading figure in this town centre transformation was Sir James Marshall. He became a member of the council in 1928 and was described in the *Croydon Times* a few years later as one of Croydon's 'men of mark ... Economy is his watchword.' He became an alderman in 1936, a magistrate in 1937, and chairman of the Whitgift Foundation in 1944. As leader of the council through the early years of redevelopment, he was directly involved with many of the schemes, including the Whitgift Centre. He was described by Peter Saunders in *Urban Politics*:

> Although an elected representative rather than an official, this hard-headed autocrat was in a sense comparable to an American-style town boss. What Marshall said, went. Extremely commercially minded and an orthodox conservative, he was, as it were, the managing director of Croydon. He got things done quickly and they

143 *(facing page)   This map shows the periods when building development took place across the borough. It should be used only as a rough guide because of the small scale.*

worked ... A property developer who had operated in Croydon recalled that, 'One didn't get anywhere if Sir James disapproved of one'.

In 1965 Croydon lost its cherished county borough status and was merged with the Coulsdon and Purley Urban District to form a London borough. Relations with the new Greater London Council (GLC) over planning issues deteriorated as attempts were made by that authority to limit office development in the town. In 1974 the GLC announced that no further office development was to be allowed in Croydon but the council persisted in allying itself with the interests of developers. This was partly due to a desire to increase rateable value and keep the rates as low as possible. In many cases quality of development was sacrificed for quantity.

There was a further mini-boom in office development during the 1980s and by the end of that decade there was over eight million square feet of office space in the town centre. Since then several of the large office blocks, including Essex House, have been demolished as they are not suitable for modern technology. Several have been adapted for residential use and one has been converted into a hotel, *Jury's Inn*, which opened in 2002.

The new developments in the town centre inevitably led to the loss of some historically and architecturally interesting buildings. In common with so many 1960s town centre developments, road building was of high priority and environmental concerns were low. There is little doubt that a more pleasant town centre could have resulted had the council developed a master scheme and sought planning gain as well as immediate financial advantage. However, the overall benefits in new shopping areas and local employment were immense. In retrospect the 1960s can be seen as a reaction to the days of war, signalling a new beginning and fresh start. It was only later that a general feeling of dissatisfaction with the drab architecture set in and the qualities of Victorian and later architecture were appreciated. Local amenity groups such as the Norwood Society and the Croydon Society were established to try to influence local politicians into taking a greater interest in the townscape and the environment generally.

During the 1970s and 1980s the council's desire to keep the level of rates low led to general deterioration in the town centre. Rate-capping had been introduced and low-spending authorities like Croydon suffered as a result. By the mid-1980s a more

145 (left)   Crown Hill was still paved with stone setts in June 1957. The Civic Hall (entrance on the right), formerly the North End Brotherhood Hall, was bought by Croydon Corporation at the beginning of the Second World War and used as the main concert hall for the town until Fairfield Halls opened in 1962. The Georgian houses between there and the Hippodrome Cinema (formerly the Theatre Royal) are those in the 1821 drawing of Crown Hill on page 48.

146 (middle)   The Purley Way industrial area was probably at its busiest in the 1950s. This aerial view shows Waddon Mill and part of the mill pond which was filled and made into a car park in the 1960s. The River Wandle is visible as it flows from Wandle Park under Purley Way to the mill. This section of river was put in a culvert in the mid-1960s. Waterman's Dry Cleaners is in the left foreground next to the Trojan Factory. Commerce Way is at the top right. Most of the factories in Purley Way are now used as warehouses or retail outlets.

147 (right)   Trolleybuses had replaced the trams on the Crystal Palace, Sutton and Mitcham routes between 1935 and 1937. The Second World War delayed the conversion of the remaining local tram routes until 1951, and then it was to motor buses. London Transport replaced the trolleybuses with motor buses too between 1959 and 1960. A route 654 trolleybus is here passing Reeves' furniture store in Church Street around 1958.

enlightened attitude eased the situation. Conditions throughout the area have improved since it was appreciated that the town was losing some of its prestige as a major shopping and commercial centre. The growing problems of traffic congestion and

148 *Sir James Marshall was born in 1895 and was a member of the council from 1928 until 1968. He was Mayor during the year 1945/6. He was knighted in 1953 and masterminded the redevelopment of the town centre during the post-war period. He died in 1979.*

pollution as a result of increased car use were at first seen as needing new roads. The council planned a town centre ring-road, of which Wellesley Road, the underpass, Park Lane, the High Street and Old Town Flyover and Old Town/Roman Way form

about two thirds. Attitudes to road building having changed and there is now little prospect that the northern part (Sumner Road/St James's Road) will be built.

The general decline in industry has adversely affected the town. Many of the factories in the Purley Way area have closed and a large out-of-town shopping area has grown up, replacing the factories. Companies such as Habitat and Halford's have closed their town centre branches and moved to this area. The huge IKEA store has been built next to the Croydon 'B' Power Station site, its two tall chimneys having been retained by the store as a landmark.

In the town centre two of the three large department stores changed in character. Allders was greatly extended and improved and now claims to be the third largest department store in the country. The owning group has branches in many parts of the country, and for a time also operated airport shops around the world. Joshua Allder, the founder, could not have foreseen how his name would become so well-known! Kennards became something of a local institution. Under the management of Robert Driscoll the store had become famous in the 1930s for its innovative style. Shetland ponies

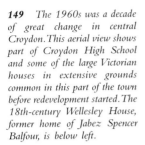

149 *The 1960s was a decade of great change in central Croydon. This aerial view shows part of Croydon High School and some of the large Victorian houses in extensive grounds common in this part of the town before redevelopment started. The 18th-century Wellesley House, former home of Jabez Spencer Balfour, is below left.*

150 *The Whitgift Shopping Centre was completed in the 1960s and soon proved very popular. In the 1980s and early 1990s the rather drab architecture was transformed and is now entirely under cover, looking very different from this view.*

gave rides to children at the Frith Road end of its arcade. There was a zoo and a large restaurant complete with Ida Santerelli and her Ladies Broadcasting Orchestra. Many events were arranged to attract customers. The store was taken over by Debenhams and its highly individual character was lost after rebuilding in the 1970s. The former large site is now partly occupied by the Drummond Centre. The other large store was Grant's, which remained a family business (sometimes a weakness in the world of modern retailing) until about 1980. It was sold and subsequently closed. The building remained in a run-down state for about 15 years, certainly not helping the image of the town centre. The splendid Victorian frontage has recently been restored as part of an otherwise complete rebuilding.

A number of well-known local businesses such as Ebbutt's, Hammond and Hussey's, Stockwell and Oxford's and Wilson's succumbed from the 1970s onwards. Sainsbury's opened their first out of London store in London Road in 1882 and within a few years had four branches in the town. The first branch was converted by the company into their first self-service store in 1950 – a landmark in shopping habits.

On the housing front much happened during this period. Soon after the war the council began more new development at New Addington, where there was plenty of land available. Alongside some temporary housing they erected a large hoarding which somewhat insensitively proclaimed 'Croydon Corporation Compound'! During the 1947 winter the estate gained the nickname of 'Little Siberia'. Much of the remaining farmland was covered with new houses, schools and factories over the ensuing decades until the isolated township had a population of about twenty-five thousand.

In 1955 the Royal Russell School appealed successfully to the Ministry of Housing and Local Government for permission to build on Ballards Farm, which formed part of its estate. Croydon Council had turned the application down and there was considerable opposition locally to the loss of what was described as 'Croydon's piece of Devon'. However, housing needs were paramount at the time and an estate was built on the attractive farmland.

Many of the large Victorian houses in Upper Norwood and at Park Hill were on 99-year leases and these began to reach maturity in the 1960s. The houses were generally well-built but too large for modern needs, having been intended for people who could afford not only the upkeep but the staff necessary to keep the properties in good order. The large gardens were ideal plots for flats or small groups of houses. Park Hill was redeveloped comprehensively in the 1960s by Wates to form Park Hill Village. This even has its own general shop and church (St Matthew's), replacing the building on its former site in George Street. Redevelopment in Upper Norwood and elsewhere has been on a much more piecemeal basis and, rather sadly, several buildings of character and quality have been replaced by indifferent architecture.

Another large-scale development by Wates was at Forestdale, Addington. The area lay between Selsdon Wood, Addington Road and Featherbed Lane. After the First World War it had been used for small-holdings, but the land was not very productive and was known locally as 'Hungry Bottom'. It has been attractively laid out with many trees and grassy

151   Inevitably the town centre redevelopment resulted in the loss of some interesting buildings. The former Nalder & Collyer Brewery buildings in the High Street dated partly from the 18th century and were photographed here in 1964 just before demolition. Leon House now occupies the site and is not a visual improvement.

banks, the houses being grouped in clusters. A large-scale housing scheme was undertaken by Croydon Council in the 1960s at Handcroft Road. This involved the wholesale clearance of mainly small Victorian houses in a number of roads between Tamworth, Mitcham and Handcroft Roads. Many of the old houses had character and today would probably be renovated but at the time wholesale replacement was seen as the key to regenerating an area. Unfortunately quite a lot of the new properties have had structural problems. More recent redevelopment schemes have been by housing associations and are on a much smaller scale.

Many of the small local factories, workshops and laundries that were scattered about the town have closed as they have ceased operations or had large companies buy them up and centralise their operations. In the 1950s vans and lorries could be seen all over the town bearing the names of local companies such as Hall & Company, Allen's Flour Mills, Woodside Brickworks, Trojan Motors and a host of others. Today most have gone and been replaced by small pockets of residential development or warehouses.

Population growth after the Second World War, and requirements for higher standards, led to a massive school building programme in the 1960s and '70s. Some of the older buildings were replaced either on the existing or on new sites. The year 1971 brought an end to the selection procedure in Croydon and all the local education authority schools became comprehensive. By the 1970s pupil numbers had begun to fall and several long-established schools were closed, the sites being used for housing or other purposes. Meanwhile Roman Catholic schools expanded as did the well-resourced private schools. There have, too, been great changes in church-going. Several parishes have amalgamated and church buildings needing expensive renovation

152   The Surrey Garden Village Trust purchased 300 acres of land, formerly a pheasant shoot, at Selsdon Vale in 1923. The land was intended for 'persons who wished to live in semi-rural surroundings and supplement their income by agricultural or horticultural pursuits'. The area was typical of many such 'plotlands' of the period with unmade roads and temporary buildings. Wates and Wimpey developed the area for housing in the 1970s and '80s. This is one of the small-holdings at Selsdon Vale in about 1970.

153   Most of the large 1860s houses on the Park Hill estate were bought by Wates on the termination of their 99-year leases and the area was comprehensively redeveloped as Park Hill Village. This view shows part of Turnpike Link in 2002.

154 *Croydon 'B' Power Station was commenced by Croydon Corporation and completed by the nationalised electricity undertaking. By the 1980s it was redundant and was closed. A scheme to use this rather fine brick building for other purposes foundered and it was demolished. The chimneys remain as a landmark for the huge IKEA store and the fields seen here in 1987 have now been used for part of the commercial development of the area.*

have in several cases been demolished, church activities taking place in the church hall or smaller purpose-built structures.

Croydon has become a much more cosmopolitan town since the 1950s. One of the greatest social changes has been the large number of immigrants who have made their home here. A large proportion have settled in the northern parts of the borough. This ethnic diversity has greatly enriched the life of the town and many new cultural and special interest groups have been formed as a result. New churches, mosques and meeting places have been built.

In 1983 Croydon celebrated the centenary of the borough charter. The old police station in Fell Road was replaced by a new one in Park Lane. The Town Hall Gardens were extended over the old

site, and formally opened and named the Queen's Gardens by the Queen as part of the royal visit to celebrate the occasion.

In the same year, the railway line between Woodside and Selsdon was closed as it carried very little traffic and had for some years only seen a few trains in peak hours. It was, though, to play an important part in the new light rail system which was planned over the next few years. The Croydon Tramlink Bill was deposited in Parliament in 1991, and the Act received Royal Assent in 1994. The scheme involved the closure in 1997 of the Elmers End/Addiscombe and West Croydon/Wimbledon railway lines. Part of the former and most of the latter were converted to light railways, and linked by new sections of on-street tramway across the town centre, with new lines to Beckenham and

155 *Norwood Grove dates from the early 19th century and typifies the country houses that once occupied an important place in the local area. The house and land were acquired by Croydon Corporation and the estate was opened as a park in 1926. There are splendid views over Croydon.*

156 *(below)   The 1890s redevelopment of the medieval market area left a few old buildings remaining in Surrey Street, and in a short section of Bell Hill, seen here in 2001. The wooden jettied building on the right dates from the 17th and 18th centuries, as does the building beyond which is faced with mathematical tiles. These have the appearance of bricks but are much lighter and cheaper. There is a building in Surrey Street which uses similar tiles.*

New Addington. Construction started in 1997 and for a couple of years local residents could watch the largest local construction project since the railways were first built. There was some local opposition in the form of an organisation called 'Tramstop' but the lines opened in May 2000. They provide a useful east-west link across the town as well as a connection between the town centre and the Purley Way shopping areas. Extensions are under consideration.

In the mid-1980s there was local controversy over plans by the Church of England to remove Croydon from the Diocese of Canterbury and merge it into the Diocese of Southwark. In administrative terms this made sense, as Croydon was the only place in the country geographically separate from the diocese to which it belonged. Also parts of the borough were already in Southwark. However, the council was opposed to the loss of

the historic link with Canterbury and a rift developed between Church and council, the Bishop and the town's civic leaders holding different opinions. In 1985 the Church won but, as a senior council official put it, 'Why should administrative convenience take precedence over long history?'.

The 1990s saw a great increase in the number of restaurants, clubs, bars and pubs in the town centre with a consequent influx of people in the evenings. New flats are being built in the town centre to ensure there is a good mix of homes, offices and shops. The imaginative 'Skyline' lighting project for some of the town centre buildings has greatly improved the appearance of the town after dark.

In 2002 the new extension to the Drummond Centre – Croydon Centrale – is under construction and will increase the area of shops. Rival plans for Park Place and Bishops Court are being considered and the council has hopes for a new 'Gateway Arena' at East Croydon. As in the 1960s, cranes are again rising around the centre; Croydon has been changing for centuries and continues to do so.

At the beginning of the 21st century it has many of the advantages and disadvantages of most large towns. With a thriving shopping and commercial centre, the problems of traffic congestion and pollution are difficult to resolve. Some manufacturing and commercial companies prefer to relocate to 'Green Field' sites where access by car and parking facilities are better. The town has excellent public transport links, which must in the long run be one of its major assets, but perhaps half of the buildings throughout the borough are now well over 80 years old, with many over 130 years old. There are areas of social deprivation and poverty as in the past, but there are also more than 3,500 local voluntary organisations with some 50,000 members. They are looked after by Croydon Voluntary Action, founded in 1907 and among the oldest umbrella bodies for voluntary groups in the UK.

There are now over 120 parks and open spaces owned by the council in the borough, covering about 2,640 acres. In addition several large areas of downland and common land are under the control

157   Boswell Court is one of the best remaining Georgian houses in the town centre and was photographed here in November 2001.

158   *This 1991 aerial view shows the striking city-scale architecture of the town centre. The Fairfield Halls, Croydon College and the Law Courts are in the centre foreground. But despite its modern appearance Croydon is largely a product of the Victorian era and fortunately some of the best of the town centre buildings from that period survive with even earlier and later architecture to remind us of the town's historic development.*

of the City of London Corporation. They were acquired in the 19th century when there was concern over the spread of Croydon into the adjacent countryside. Despite 200 years of urban development there are still areas of attractive open land within a mile or so of the town centre. The old estates of Coombe, Coombe Farm, Heathfield and Ballards, with the Addington Hills and Croham Hurst, and several golf courses, are valued remnants of the countryside which once covered virtually the whole of the present borough.

The council was instrumental in setting up the Edge Cities Network, linking half a dozen major self-contained areas on the edge of their respective national capitals. From Espoo in Finland and Nacka in Sweden, to Fingal outside Belfast and Kifissia on the edge of Athens, these areas worked together to pool experiences and bid, successfully, for European Union funding. Croydon has unsuccessfully sought city status several times in recent years. It is a city in all but name and the council has developed its '2020 Vision' of how the town could develop in the first decades of the new century. It is certain that there will be no shortage of new challenges to be faced and new problems to be overcome.

Some Significant Dates in Croydon's History

809	Church Synod held at Croydon.
960	Elfsies, Priest of Croydon.
1086	Domesday Book records Croydon, Waddon, Coulsdon, Watendone, Addington and Sanderstead.
1229	First recorded visit of a King – Henry III.
1264	Skirmish between King's and Simon de Montfort's men at Norbury.
1273/6	Archbishop Kilwardby obtained charter for a market every Wednesday and a fair to be held for nine days from 16 May.
1286	Lord William de Warrenne slain in a tournament at Duppas Hill.
1343	Archbishop Stratford obtained a grant for a market on Saturdays, and a Fair.
1409	King James I of Scotland imprisoned at Croydon House.
1533	John Frith tried for heresy by Archbishop Cranmer.
1556	Queen Mary held 23 Privy Council meetings in Croydon.
1573	Queen Elizabeth I held a Privy Council meeting.
1585/1588	Queen Elizabeth I attended horse racing at Croydon.
1599	Whitgift Hospital completed.
1691	First petition for Incorporation as a Borough
1707	Another petition for Incorporation submitted and approved but for some reason not implemented.
1718	First turnpike road through the town.
1727	Workhouse built on Duppas Hill.
1794	Barracks established at Pitlake.
1797	Croydon Enclosure Act passed.
1801	Croydon Enclosure Award published.
1803	Surrey Iron Railway opened from Wandsworth to Croydon.
1805	Croydon, Merstham & Godstone Iron Railway opened to Merstham.
1809	Croydon Canal opened.
	East India Company's college at Addiscombe opened.
	Second Town Hall and Butter Market opened.
1825	Friends School moved from Islington to Croydon.
1827	Gas works established.
1829	Improvement Commissioners established.
	Parish divided. New churches are All Saints', Upper Norwood and St James's, Croydon Common.
1831	Beulah Spa opened.
1836	Croydon Board of Guardians set up.
	Croydon Canal closed.
1838	Croydon, Merstham & Godstone Iron Railway closed.
1839	London & Croydon Railway opened (to West Croydon).
1841	London and Brighton railway opened (via East Croydon).
1842	South Eastern Railway to Dover via Redhill opened.
1846	Experiment with atmospheric traction on Croydon railway.
	Surrey Iron Railway closed.
1849	Inquiry into water and sewage under Public Health Act.
1850	Local Board of Health set up.
	Cattle Market opened at Selsdon Road.
1851	Waterworks in Surrey Street opened.
1854	Crystal Palace opened just beyond Croydon boundary.
1855	*Croydon Chronicle* first published.
1858	Beulah Spa closed.
1861	Addiscombe Military College closed.
	Croydon Times first published.
1865	New Workhouse opened at Queen's Road.
1867	Parish church almost completely destroyed by fire.

1869   *Croydon Advertiser* first published.
1870   Croydon Natural History and Scientific Society formed (as Croydon Microscopical Club).
        Rebuilt Croydon Parish church consecrated.
1871   Croydon School Board established.
        First holiday (August) under Bank Holidays Act.
1875   Bath and West of England Agricultural Show held at Waddon.
1879   Friends School closed on removal to Saffron Walden.
        First section of horse tramways opened.
1883   Charter of Incorporation as a Borough granted.
        Local Board of Health disbanded.
1885   New Infirmary opened at Mayday Road (now Mayday Hospital).
        Croydon's first MP elected (Mr W. Grantham).
1887   Croydon ceased to be an Assize town.
1888   Croydon became a County Borough.
1890   Croydon Camera Club formed.
        Croydon Public Libraries established.
1891   Croydon Polytechnic opened at Scarbrook Road.
1893   Work started on clearing the Middle Row area.
1894   Croydon Rural District Council formed, comprising the parishes of Addington, Beddington, Coulsdon,
        Merton, Mitcham, Morden, Penge, Sanderstead, Wallington and Woodmansterne.
1896   New Town Hall opened.
        Electricity works opened and electric street lighting inaugurated in town centre.
1901   Electric tramway opened between Norbury and Purley.
        Bath and West of England Show held at Addiscombe.
1904   Opening of Stanley Halls, South Norwood.
1915   Coulsdon & Purley Urban District Council formed.
        Croydon Rural District Council abolished.
1918   National Aircraft Factory Number One and Waddon test airfield opened.
1920   Croydon Airport became the Official Air Terminus for London.
1923   Southern Railway formed to include local railways.
1925   Purley Way opened as town by-pass.
1928   Addington became part of Croydon borough.
        New Croydon Airport Terminal and hotel opened.
1930   Croydon Guardians ceased to exist.
1933   London Passenger Transport Board formed and took over local tram and bus services.
1935   Work started on building at New Addington.
        Cattle Market in Selsdon Road closed.
1936   Crystal Palace destroyed by fire.
1940   Croydon Airport bombed in first air raid on London area during Second World War.
1948   Croydon hospitals became part of National Health Service.
        Croydon Gas Company nationalised.
        Croydon Electricity Undertaking nationalised.
1951   Last tram ran in Croydon.
1954   The last local brewery, Page & Overton's, closed.
        Royal School of Church Music moved to Addington Palace.
1956   Croydon Corporation Act passed permitting redevelopment
        of town centre.
1959   Grand and Davis Theatres and Eros Cinema closed.
        Croydon Airport closed.
        First part of town centre redevelopment – Norfolk House opened.
1960   Croydon Millennary celebrations.
1961   Lanfranc air disaster – 34 children and two teachers killed.
1962   Fairfield Halls opened.
1965   Croydon ceased to be a county borough on merger with
        Coulsdon and Purley to form a London Borough.
1966   Whitgift Shopping Centre opened.
1967   *Croydon Times* ceased publication after 106 years.
        High Street and Old Town flyover opened.
1983   Centenary of Borough celebrated with Royal visit.
1985   Croydon removed from Diocese of Canterbury and included in Southwark Diocese.
1993   Clocktower complex, museum and new library opened.
1996   Whitgift Foundation celebrated 400th anniversary.
        Royal visit.
2000   Croydon Tramlink opened.

Bibliography

Anderson, J. Corbet, *A Short Chronicle concerning the Parish of Croydon* (Reeves and Turner, 1882)

Anderson, J. Corbet, *Croydon Inclosure* (Blades, East and Blades, 1889)

Anderson, J. Corbet, *Chronicles of the Parish of Croydon, Surrey* (1874)

Baddeley, G.E., *The Tramways of Croydon* (Light Rail Transit Association, 1983)

Bannerman, Ronald, *Forgotten Croydon* (Croydon Times, 1945)

Bayliss, Derek A., *Retracing the First Public Railway* (Living History Publications, 1985)

Beaver, Patrick, *The Crystal Palace* (Phillimore, 1986)

Beavis, Jim, *The Croydon Races* (Local History Publications, 1999)

Berwick Sayers, W.C., *Samuel Coleridge Taylor – Musician – his Life and Letters* (Cassell, 1915)

Berwick Sayers, W.C. (ed.), *Croydon and the Second World War* (The Croydon Corporation, 1949)

Blair, John, *Early Medieval Surrey* (Alan Sutton Publishing and Surrey Archaeological Society, 1991)

Broadbent, U. and Latham, R., *Coulsdon Downland Village* (Bourne Society, 1976)

Canning and Clyde Road Residents' Association and Friends, *The Book of Addiscombe* (Halsgrove, 2001)

Cluett, Douglas (ed.), Learmonth, Bob and Bogle, Joanna, *The First Croydon Airport, 1915-1928* (Croydon Airport Society, 2nd edition, 2001)

Cluett, Douglas, Nash, Joanna and Learmonth, Bob, *Croydon Airport: The Great Days 1928-1939* (Sutton Libraries and Arts Services 1980)

Coulter, John, *Norwood Past* (H.P.L., 1996)

Cox, R.C.W., 'Some Aspects of the Urban Development of Croydon' (unpublished thesis, 1966)

Croydon Advertiser, *Jesse Ward* (Croydon Advertiser, 1951)

Croydon Society and Croydon Council, *Croydon's Built Heritage* (Croydon Society and Croydon Council, 1995)

Dobson, C.G., *A Century and a Quarter* (Hall Co., 1951)

Ducarel, Dr, *Some Account of the Town, Church and Archiepiscopal Palace of Croydon* (J. Nicholls, 1783)

Farries, K.G. and Mason, M.T., *The Windmills of Surrey and Inner London* (Charles Skilton, 1966)

Frost, Thomas, *Forty Years Recollections, Literary and Political* (1880)

Frost, Thomas, *Reminiscences of a Country Journalist* (1886)

Gadsby, Joy, *Village Histories 3: Sanderstead* (Bourne Society, 1998)

Garrow, the Rev D.W., *The History and Antiquities of Croydon* (W. Annan, 1818)

Gent, John B., *Croydon: A Pictorial History* (Phillimore, 1991)

Gent, John B. (ed.), *Croydon between the Wars* (Croydon Natural History and Scientific Society, 1992)

Gent, John B. (ed.), *Croydon from Above* (Croydon Natural History and Scientific Society, 1999)

Gent, John B. (ed.), *Croydon in the 1940s and 1950s* (Croydon Natural History and Scientific Society, 1994)

Gent, John B. (ed.), *Croydon Old and New* (Croydon Natural History and Scientific Society, 1996)

Gent, John B. (ed.), *Croydon: The Story of a Hundred Years* (Croydon Natural History and Scientific Society, 1988)

Gent, John B. (ed.), *Croydon's Transport through the Ages* (Croydon Natural History and Scientific Society, 2001)

Gent, John B. (ed.), *Edwardian Croydon Illustrated* (Croydon Natural History and Scientific Society, 1990)

Gent, John B. (ed.), *Victorian Croydon Illustrated* (Croydon Natural History and Scientific Society, 1987)

Higham, A., *Village Histories 1: Purley* (Bourne Society, 1996)

Hobbs, Doris C.H., *The Croydon Police 1829-1840* (Croydon Natural History and Scientific Society Proceedings, vol.17, Part 6, April 1983)

Lancaster, Brian, *Croydon Church Townscape* (Croydon Natural History and Scientific Society, 1997)

Lancaster, Brian, *The Croydon Case: Dirty Old Town to Model Town* (Croydon Natural History and Scientific Society, 2001)

Living History Guide No.1, *Central Croydon* (Living History Publications, 1978)

Living History Guide No.2, *Coombe, Shirley and Addington* (Living History Publications, 1985)

Living History Guide No.6, *Selsdon and Croham* (Living History Publications, 1983)

Living History Guide No.7, *Retracing Canals to Croydon and Camberwell* (Living History Publications, 1986)

Lovett, Vivien, *Kennards of Croydon* (Vivien Whitehouse, 2000)

Lovett, Vivien, *Surrey Street Croydon* (Vivien Whitehouse, 1995)

Maggs, Ken and DeAthe, Paul, *The Roman Roads of East Surrey and the Kent Border* (North Downs Press, 1987)

Marshall, W., *Minutes of Agriculture on a Farm near Croydon* (1788)

McInnes, P., Sparkes, B., and Broderick, P., *Croydon at Work* (Croydon Society and Croydon Chamber of Commerce and Industry, 1991)

Moore, H. Keatley and Berwick Sayers, W.C., *Croydon and the Great War* (Corporation of Croydon, 1920)

Morris, Jeremy, *Religion and Urban Change – Croydon 1840-1914* (Royal Historical Society, 1992)

Paget, Clarence G., *Byways in the History of Croydon* (Croydon Public Libraries, 1929)

Paget, Clarence G., *Croydon Homes of the Past* (Croydon Public Libraries, 1937)

Pelton, John Ollis, *Relics of Old Croydon* (Roffey and Clark, 1891)

Percy, F.H.G., *Whitgift School: A History* (The Whitgift Foundation, 1991)

Saunders, Peter, *Urban Politics* (1991)

Scales, Ian, *Village Histories 5: Coulsdon* (Bourne Society, 2000)

Skinner, M.W.G., *Croydon's Railways* (Kingfisher Railway Productions, 1985)

Steinman, G. Steinman, *A History of Croydon* (Longman, 1833)

Steward, Michael, Gent, John and Stannard, Colin, *Tramlink Official Handbook* (Capital Transport, 2000)

Stone, Patricia, *Ragged, British, Quaker, Soldier – Nineteenth Century Croydon Schools* (AMCD, 1992)

Thornhill, Lilian, *From Palace to Washhouse* (Croydon Natural History and Scientific Society, Proceedings, vol.17, Part 9, June 1987)

Thornhill, Lilian, *Woodside* (North Downs Press, 1986)

Turner, J.T. Howard, *The London, Brighton and South Coast Railway, Vol.1: Origins and Formation* (Batsford, 1977)

Turner, J.T. Howard, *The London, Brighton and South Coast Railway, Vol.2: Establishment and Growth* (Batsford, 1978)

Turner, J.T. Howard, *The London, Brighton and South Coast Railway, Vol.3: Completion and Maturity* (Batsford, 1979)

Vibart, H.M., *Addiscombe: Its Heroes and Men of Note* (Archibald Constable, 1894)

Warren, Frank, *Addington: A History* (Phillimore, 1984)

Warwick, Alan, *The Phoenix Suburb* (The Norwood Society, 1991)

Webb, William, *Garden First in Land Development* (reprinted 1986 on behalf of Webb Estate Society)

Winterman, M.A., *Croydon's Parks: An Illustrated History* (Parks and Recreation Department, Croydon, 1988)

There are numerous other useful publications including local directories and newsapers, volumes of old photographs, transport books by Middleton Press, and articles in publications of the Bourne Society and the Croydon Natural History and Scientific Society. Croydon Local Studies Library in the Clocktower, Katharine Street holds copies of most of these and many other books and publications of local interest which are very useful to anyone wishing to undertake further research.

Index

Numbers in **bold** indicate page references to illustrations.